TOGAF® 10 Level 2

Enterprise Arch

Part 2 Exam

Scenario Questions

Scenario Strategies

Wonder Guide

Volume 2

Covers many questions, reasoning of answers

More than that, the Strategy to get all of them right

Note that TOGAF® 10 has an upgraded syllabus content that spans into the Core document - TOGAF® Standard Fundamental Content Version 10 and also into a few Series Guides that are added in the Exam Conformance list.

Thus, the knowledge base with it is broader, with a number of state-of-art topics well highlighted through the Series Guides.

We have taken care of referring to those contents from Series Guides that seem to be important for TOGAF® 10 Certification, in the questions and discussions in this Book as also in all other Books of this TOGAF® 10 Series. This Volume 2 - Scenario Strategies Book gets more into questions related to Series Guides that align with ADM and other TOGAF® topics.

Inspirations for questions have come from various internet sources, including mock tests and sample questions. We thank all those behind this effort and appreciate their role in helping all those who want to get TOGAF® Certified.

We recommend that after understanding the strategy in approaching the Level 2 questions from this Book Series, all should also subsequently attempt the various on-line timed tests and also go through various e-Books and print books available with sample questions. These are available on a free or commercial basis.

Cartoon images are added to add value and for ease of reading and learning, cutting out the monotony.

Our thanks extend to public domain images from publicdomainvectors.org.

All Trademarks and TOGAF® including Boundaryless Information Flow™ are respected and is implied to have applied where applicable.

Points in **regular bold** are positive and ones in ***italics bold*** are negative

SQ 201

You are the Chief Enterprise Architect for a large financial institution. You are supported by a group of Segment Architects with broad expertise as also by a set of Solutions Architects who have specific domain expertise with B D A T respectively. Your Team also has experience in coordinating and working with LOB – Line Of Business through the Strategic Planners, with PMO, the corporate Project Management Office and also with Operations Management.

The institution has a long standing history of nearly 70 years in banking and related areas. They have started in modest strength but have grown both organically and also through many acquisitions. Their IT portfolio is currently enriched with more than 100 running projects. Nevertheless the Top Management through the Governing Board has asked to set a goal towards a more structured approach to its infrastructure and service. The driving elements behind the goals is the necessity for caution in the business environment seen in light of imbalances in the financial system and volatility in global economic scenario, duly caused by wars and other geopolitical events.

The CIO has sponsored the creation of such an enterprise architecture group as described above. Your group has adopted TOGAF® version 10 as the basic framework for enterprise architecture. So far an Architecture Vision has been developed and got approved. Thereafter the Team ensured the definition of a suitable and appropriate set of domain architectures. The stage in ADM is now poised to consolidate the domain architectures. The idea is to further review the consolidated work and create new project proposals that are solution centric and which will realize the vision.

The CIO has expressed that even though physical implementation is to be carried out by other change Agents and not EA department, the implementation approach taken up now has to look at current and futuristic opportunities that are open to us in an environment of envisaged changes in the technology and business landscapes. All Stakeholders who will be exposed with the work done now for comments may want to see the vision being taken forward to a flexible, integrated Implementation and Migration Plan that has the best chance of realizing the vision in these uncertain times.

What are the recommendations towards such an approach that you would like to give to your Team ?

Based on TOGAF®, find out as to which of the following would be the best answer ?

A : Your recommendation suggests that the EA Team will look into all of the existing projects along with whatever has been their deliverables. This leads to looking into the findings from the Gap Analysis results for the four architecture domains, based on the B D A T work so far. The Team will also be in close communication with the various stakeholders and obtain the details of all existing project architectures. This will enable the EA Team towards smoother integration and with due coherence. The operations management will also be involved and informed likewise so that they can prepare to support the deliverables.

Thus the Domain Architects are made to work in coordination with each other and with the Segment Architect. They will all sit together, come up with specific newer projects which are meant to address the gaps. This goes side by side with the question of whether existing projects need to undergo some revision in their scope. In this way, the net total work required in each of the domains will then be funnelled into the Implementation and Migration Plan. Alongside, the timeline for progress of deliverables on the implementation tasks will be documented in the Architecture Roadmap.

While working towards such details and the work package, your Team identified exact areas where a solution may have to be invented and create new work packages. They have also suggested proof-of-concept validations before the implementation could scale out in selected areas. The main focus of the Architecture is now to Support Portfolio. This approach has to maximize the mileage gained while still constrained with available resources. The additional focus is to identify conditions under which projected mileage gain is achievable. The third level of focus is to identify barriers to achieve the goal and build efforts to diminish the impact of such barriers. The final objective is to provide an assurance of investment to result in appropriate risk-reward ratio. You looked into the work of the Team and ensured that they populated the list of projects required to meet these four objectives. This was done by looking at the effort and resource estimates for all work packages. This also necessitated a revisit of the dependencies across work packages.

B : You go with a recommendation that all the domain architectures as completed so far are implemented immediately. Your recommendation further suggests that all in-flight projects should undergo a scope revision exercise. Such an action is essential to align them with the new architectures.

Since time is the essence, you will run the requirements from Phases B through D and create new IT projects corresponding to each one of the requirements. Such an action enables the portfolios to be created in line with their individual requirements-based project architectures.

The projects will, after such actions, is expected to work together through the creation of new point-to-point interfaces. This is to be in line with defined interoperability architecture guidelines.

You examined, before making the recommendation, about what is achievable and identified logical work packages that can become the basis for projects or the leveraging of existing projects. The main focus of the Architecture now to Support Portfolio was to maximize the mileage gained with available resources. The second objective is to identify conditions under with projected mileage gain is achievable. The third is to identify barriers to achieve the goal and build efforts to diminish the impact of such barriers. The final objective is to provide assurance of investment to reward ratio being unaltered. You populated the list of projects required to meet these four objectives, by gathering the effort and resource estimates for all work packages. You revisited the dependencies across work packages.

C : You strongly recommended the focus to be on the development of a series of Transition Architectures. These Transitions Architectures are to be carefully planned to deliver continuous business value in an incremental manner. Such a continuous business value target can be achieved by making sure that all the projects deliver their increments in a well-knit approach. This will meet the third partition of the Architecture Landscape, namely capability planning resulting in capability architecture. Hence your recommendation was to consolidate the Gap Analysis results from each of the domain architectures, with due analysis of the dependencies and thus come up with a work-breakdown structure.

You suggested that the Team examines what is achievable and to use the result of such an examination to identify logical work packages. This can become the basis for newer projects as also the take-off based on existing projects. SBBs are to be created accordingly.

You proposed a series of sessions to seek comments and the after consensus on the Implementation and Migration Strategy. In the recommendation to proceed towards the preparation of the work package, you suggested that the Team identifies pockets where a solution may have to be invented and hereby to create new work packages. These are to be used (at the physical implementation stage) to perform proof-of-concept validations, where necessary, before they could scale out.

The main focus of the Architecture that is to Support Portfolio was to maximize the mileage gained with available resources. The second objective is to identify conditions under with projected mileage gain is achievable. The third is to identify barriers to achieve the goal and build efforts to diminish the impact of such barriers. The final objective is to provide assurance of investment to reward ratio being unaltered. You point to these objectives to the Team and asked them to populate the list of projects required to meet these four objectives, by gathering the effort and resource estimates for all work packages. You revisited the dependencies across work packages after such a work completion.

D : Your recommendation was that the stakeholders alone come up with ideas and inputs on what has to be done to implement the defined domain architectures. This democratizes the stakeholders contribution to the EA planning routine. Such a coordinated exercises will have the outcome of an item wise list of work activities. This is sufficient to arrive at an IT portfolio plan that will suggest a series of projects. They will have a comprehensive Target Architecture that can give directions of a long term initiative such as next three years. The report will include a detailed dependencies and factors assessment.

You examined what is achievable and identified logical work packages that can become the basis for projects or the leveraging of existing projects. The main focus of the Architecture now to Support Portfolio was to maximize the mileage gained with available resources. The second objective is to identify conditions under with projected mileage gain is achievable. The third is to identify barriers to achieve the goal and build efforts to diminish the impact of such barriers. The final objective is to provide assurance of investment to reward ratio being unaltered. You populated the list of projects required to meet these four objectives, by gathering the effort and resource estimates for all work packages. You revisited the dependencies across work packages.

Proceeding to tackle the question and getting full five marks :

As you read the question, note the following points:

Issues in focus and the Business Context :

Major financial institution; in business for long years.

It has a large IT service department and routinely has over 100 infrastructure and service projects in progress.

Enterprise architecture group is operating.

Architecture Vision – approved.

But what Phase are in we in thereafter ?

Since it says "Defined a set of domain architectures", the scenario description clearly points out that Phases B to D are completed.

Further clues clarify that the current stage is in Phase E and not anywhere else.

Concerns : Need for a flexible, integrated Implementation and Migration Plan that has the best chance of realizing the vision in these uncertain times.

Aim : To consolidate the domain architectures and review the current initiatives and projects in the corporate portfolio as well as potentially create new projects in order to realize the vision.

To do :

To recommend the best approach to address the concerns raised.

Phase E : Start Initial Planning for Migration and (code development) Implementation.

It is an Initial but complete version of the Architecture : Transition Architecture.

How should we approach this Scenario based question ?

We need to identify the portion of TOGAF® documentation (available online during Level 2 Exam) so that we can quickly go to that portion and focus only on that. Not more than half a minute to be spent on this search.

9. Phase E: Opportunities & Solutions

[1]

Also portions of the answer choices referred to the TOGAF® Series Guide

: **A Practitioners' Approach to Developing Enterprise Architecture**[2]

and the section therein :

A Practitioners' Approach to Developing Enterprise Architecture Following the TOGAF® ADM

[3]

8.3 Balance Opportunity and Viability

[4]

Some points from this section 8.3 reads as :

Develop the ..... Architecture specifications to the extent needed to ... for options. The focus is more on ... than ... a solution.

In elaborating the architecture, new .... will arise, and so should ....

It is time to reach into the ... for ..., and ... to develop an approach to ....

Identify pockets where a .. In such a case, create ... to perform .... before ...out. Understand .... is actually ...., not architecture

---

1. https://pubs.opengroup.org/togaf-standard/adm/chap09.html

2. https://pubs.opengroup.org/togaf-standard/adm-practitioners/index.html

3. https://pubs.opengroup.org/togaf-standard/adm-practitioners/index.html

4. https://pubs.opengroup.org/togaf-standard/adm-practitioners/adm-practitioners_8.html#_Toc95288871

The main focus of the Architecture to Support.... is to ... with available .... The second objective is ..... The third is to ..... The final objective is to ...

Populate ... these four objectives.

Looking at answer choice A :

Your recommendation suggests that the EA Team will look into all of the existing projects along with whatever has been their deliverables. This leads to looking into the findings from the Gap Analysis results for the four architecture domains, based on the B D A T work so far.

To go for findings from the Gap Analysis results. – **Correct**. Phase E steps requires this to happen upfront.

The Team will also be in close communication with the various stakeholders and obtain the details of all existing project architectures. This will enable the EA Team towards smoother integration and with due coherence. Partly correct. This happens more in Phase F while this scenario is fixated in Phase E

The operations management will also be involved and informed likewise so that they can prepare to support the deliverables. - This is very early in implementation action of ADM, not much of a Phase E activity. At best, some of it will happen in Phase F and more of it as an oversight in Phase G also.

Thus the Domain Architects are made to work in coordination with each other and with the Segment Architect. They will all, together, come up with specific newer projects which are meant to address the gaps. Not really. ABBs prepared so far will have to be transformed into SBBs, which is not any newer project creation. This is a less correct approach that addresses the deliverables of the architectures but in an uncoordinated way. It looks at rolling up the work in each domain rather than consolidating the gaps and creating projects as a function of capability management. It also does not directly describe the use of Transition Architecture. It does describe the role of the Implementation and Migration Plan and the Architecture Roadmap accurately.

This goes side by side with the question of whether existing projects need to undergo some revision in their scope . In this way, the net total work required in each of the domains will then be funnelled into the Implementation and Migration Plan. Alongside, the timeline for progress of deliverables on the implementation tasks will be documented in the Architecture Roadmap. Valid points

While working towards such details and the work package, your Team identified exact areas where a solution may have to be invented and created new work packages. They have also suggested proof-of-concept validations before the implementation could scale out in selected areas. The main focus of the Architecture is now to Support Portfolio. This approach has to maximize the mileage gained which is still constrained with available resources. The additional focus is to identify conditions under with projected mileage gain is achievable. The third level of focus is to identify barriers to achieve the goal and build efforts to diminish the impact of such barriers. The final objective is to provide an assurance of investment to result in appropriate risk-reward ratio. You looked into the work of the Team and ensured that they populated the list of projects required to meet these four objective. This was done by looking at the effort and resource estimates for all work packages. This also necessitated a revisit of the dependencies across work packages. Valid points. Quite in line with what we find in the Series Guide as cited above.

Looking at answer choice B :

You go with a recommendation that all the domain architectures as completed so far are implemented immediately. Your recommendation further suggests that all in-flight projects should undergo scope revision exercise. Such an action is essential to align them with the new architectures.

Since time is the essence, you will run the requirements from Phases B through D and create new IT projects corresponding to each one of the requirements. Such an action enables the portfolios to be created in line with their individual requirements-based project architectures.

The projects will, after such actions, is expected to work together through the creation of new point-to-point interfaces. This is to be in line with defined interoperability architecture guidelines.

Why are the above points marked as wrong ?

Domain architectures are implemented immediately. - Totally against ADM. ABBs, which are domain architectures, will need to be trasnfomred into SBBs well before physical implementation.

Run the requirements from Phases B through D and create new IT projects. - What happens to all work done so far ?

Projects will work together through the creation of new point-to-point interfaces. - Something of Phase G and beyond.

You examined, before making the recommendation, about what is achievable and identified logical work packages that can become the basis for projects or the leveraging of existing projects. The main focus of the Architecture now to Support Portfolio was to maximize the mileage gained with available resources. The second objective is to identify conditions under with projected mileage gain is achievable. The third is to identify barriers to achieve the goal and build efforts to diminish the impact of such barriers. The final objective is to provide assurance of investment to reward ratio being unaltered. You populated the list of projects required to meet these four objectives, by gathering the effort and resource estimates for all work packages. You revisited the dependencies across work packages. – These points may be in resonance with the Series Guide cited above, but are meaningless if proceeded after above in-correct actions are taken.

This approach does not address the concerns, nor follow TOGAF® version 10 guidance. Most likely it would produce IT-centric architectures and plans that ignore proper documentation and coordination with other stakeholders in order to deliver IT infrastructure as soon as possible. *Treat this as the distractor answer.*

Looking at answer choice C :

You strongly recommended the focus to be on the development of a series of Transition Architectures. These Transitions Architectures are to be carefully planned to deliver continuous business value in an incremental manner. Such a continuous business value target can be achieved by making sure that all the projects deliver their increments in a well-knit approach. This will meet the third partition of the Architecture Landscape, namely capability planning resulting in capability architecture. (Mention of Architecture Partitioning and its positioning as per Phase E is to be appreciated)

Hence your recommendation was to consolidate the Gap Analysis results from each of the domain architectures, with due analysis of the dependencies and thus come up with a work-breakdown structure. (Consolidation first, dependency check next and then move on to a work breakdown effort. Appears to be very proper approach)

You suggested that the Team examines what is achievable and to use the result of such an examination to identify

logical work packages. This can become the basis for newer projects as also the take-off based on existing projects. **SBBs are to be created accordingly.** (Examining the practicality towards MVP - Minimum Viable Product, using this result towards selecting SBBs to be transformed next with due consideration of existing projects – Neat approach)

You proposed a series of sessions to seek comments and thereafter due consensus on the Implementation and Migration Strategy. In the recommendation to proceed towards the preparation of the work package, you suggested that the Team identifies pockets where a solution may have to be invented and hereby to create new work packages. These are to be used (at the physical implementation stage) to perform proof-of-concept validations, where necessary, before they could scale out. (While architectural work packages are completed by the EA Team, they are to involve the agile development – operations Teams just to get their comments; the areas – pockets – where a fresh solution is appearing in the work package, these are pointed out be deployed on a linear scale first, more like a proof-of-concept before it is accepted for larger scale production operations. All these are great points)

The main focus of the Architecture that is to Support Portfolio was to maximize the mileage gained with available resources. The second objective is to identify conditions under with projected mileage gain is achievable. The third is to identify barriers to achieve the goal and build efforts to diminish the impact of such barriers. The final objective is to provide assurance of investment to reward ratio being unaltered. You point to these objectives to the Team and asked them to populate the list of projects required to meet these four objectives, by gathering the effort and resource estimates for all work packages. You revisited the dependencies across work packages after such a work completion.

Every point is in perfect tuning with version 10. The last portions are also in line with the portions of the Series Guide referred above.

This should be the best answer, provided last answer choice D does not excel over this. It recommends the use of Transition Architectures and capability increments to deliver business value which addresses the concern that the implementation has the ability to accommodate changes to technology and business landscape. It describes the migration planning techniques to deliver Transition Architectures, as well as seeking consensus input on the Implementation and Migration Strategy rather than going straight to an Implementation and Migration Plan

Looking at answer choice D :

Your recommendation was that the stakeholders alone come up with ideas and inputs on what has to be done to implement the defined domain architectures. This democratizes the stakeholders contribution to the EA planning routine. Such a coordinated exercises will have the outcome of an item wise list of work activities. This is sufficient to arrive at an IT portfolio plan that will suggest a series of projects. They will have a comprehensive Target Architecture that can give directions of a long term initiative such as next three years. The report will include a detailed dependencies and factors assessment.

You examined what is achievable and identified logical work packages that can become the basis for projects or the leveraging of existing projects. The main focus of the Architecture now to Support Portfolio was to maximize the mileage gained with available resources. The second objective is to identify conditions under which projected mileage gain is achievable. The third is to identify barriers to achieve the goal and build efforts to diminish the impact of such barriers. The final objective is to provide assurance of investment to reward ratio being unaltered. You populated the list of projects required to meet these four objectives, by gathering the effort and resource estimates for all work packages. You revisited the dependencies across work packages.

Stakeholders alone to provide input on what has to be done to implement. - This is to be done continuously from Phase A. Not just in Phase E. Inputs will have to captured from the stakeholders, but all innovative ideas of architects, based on their viewpoint approach are also kind of inputs only.

Carryout joint analysis will then result in a detailed list of work activities. - TOGAF® expects work transition planning only by the Architects. This will eventually give rise to a series of projects. Joint discussions are proposed in Phase F, by when all architecture work is completed and only general consultation on the physical (coding and installation) implementation is discussed. Only the agile developer - operations Team is invited to give comments on the SBB creation work in Phase E.

To create a comprehensive Target for the next three years. - This is done in Preliminary Phase.

Carrying out detailed dependencies and factors assessment. - OK point.

While the last paragraph, as repeated below, is in line with the portions of the Series Guide referred above, it does not make sense to say these in the contest of the wrong points mentioned above.

You examined what is achievable and identified logical work packages that can become the basis for projects or the leveraging of existing projects. The main focus of the Architecture now to Support Portfolio was to maximize the mileage gained with available resources. The second objective is to identify conditions under with projected mileage gain is achievable. The third is to identify barriers to achieve the goal and build efforts to diminish the impact of such barriers. The final objective is to provide assurance of investment to reward ratio being unaltered. You populated the list of projects required to meet these four objectives, by gathering the effort and resource estimates for all work packages. You revisited the dependencies across work packages.

This is *less correct answer choice as a whole*, as it focuses on a detailed technology-based Implementation and Migration Plan - comprehensive Target Architecture, negating the impact of using Transition Architectures to deliver incremental business value that could absorb technology and business environment change.

Conclusion and Answer :

Go through all four Observations.

Best answer : C

Second best answer : A

Third best answer : D

Distractor : B

SQ 202

You are the Chief Architect for a financial conglomerate that recently was strengthened and formed through the merging of three banking and finance companies. The operating model behind their respective businesses have been studied and brought under an umbrella system. This is the result of an enterprise architecture program which has been put in place as part of the integration of the three organizations.

The company has adopted the TOGAF® Architecture Development Method. The Architecture Board has approved the strawman (outline) Implementation and Migration Plan as produced by the ADM Phase of Opportunities and Solutions. The project proposals packed suitably as work packages are now at the stage of a detailed migration planning exercise. A working group has been formed that involves all the key architects and the stakeholders from the corporate matrix (those who will work on the project).

It is recognized that other departments outside of the enterprise architecture Team will have the responsibility to fund (provide a part of their budget), build (PMO tasks), support (Operations tasks), and use (takeover by LOB) what is put in place as the finalised Implementation and Migration plan given by the enterprise architecture Team after due approval of the Top Management. The success of this plan and its subsequent physical implementation is very important and is critical for the enterprise. This is so because of the intense competition in the marketplace duly challenged by Fintech companies and Neo banks. At the same time the Line of Business have a inherent apprehension of the newer business models and have started showing their lines of resistance

The CIO is the sponsor of the program and has expressed the desire for an incremental approach to rollout the intended integration program, one of the purpose behind it being to bring gradual levels of confidence to the LOB personnel.

You have been asked to describe :

• How you would conduct migration planning

• What you would be creating

• Who you would involve

• What would be the major deliverable(s)

Based on TOGAF® version 10, which of the following is the best answer ?

A : Migration planning should be conducted by the Chief Architect through direct reports from others and then it is shared with the domain architects. When complete, the Implementation and Migration Plan will be sent to the Architecture Board secretariat for circulation before the next meeting. The plan will include a prioritized list of projects, their approximate cost, and the recommended way ahead. Comments from the Board (and their staff) would be incorporated into the plan and then the individual projects would have to go in front of the Board to secure approval for project resources for the next project increment. The Implementation and Migration Plan would include a high-level GANT chart that could be used as the Architecture Roadmap.

Once impacts have been resolved, you had to create the views necessary to convey to the stakeholders that their concerns have been addressed with the necessary constraints and guidance developed prior to initiation of solution delivery for it to be successful. You noted that the Practitioner's job is to show that a sufficient level of scrutiny led to the deliverables of the Architecture Project for the solution delivery architecture to succeed. You should prove to the stakeholders that when the Architecture Project is consumed by the solution delivery architecture, their requirements have been met and changes to the enterprise will be guided and constrained efficiently. You thus identified and secured approval for the resources necessary to begin allocating the budget for the solution delivery architecture to begin.

B : Migration planning should be conducted by the enterprise architecture Team. The approach should be confirmed and coordinated with related management frameworks involved. Detailed resource estimates should be created for the work to be completed and the business value identified for all deliverables. A series of Transition Architectures should be planned that takes priorities into account. When this is completed the Implementation and Migration Plan can be finalized.

The Business Planning, Portfolio Management, and Operations Management groups should all be involved in the development of the major deliverables. Once the deliverables have been completed, the architecture development cycle should be completed.

Once impacts have been resolved, you had to create the views necessary to convey to the stakeholders that their concerns have been addressed with the necessary constraints and guidance developed prior to initiation of solution delivery for it to be successful. You noted that the Practitioner's job is to show that a sufficient level of scrutiny led to the deliverables of the Architecture Project for the solution delivery architecture to succeed. You should prove to the stakeholders that when the Architecture Project is consumed by the solution delivery architecture, their requirements have been met and changes to the enterprise will be guided and constrained efficiently. You thus identified and secured approval for the resources necessary to begin allocating the budget for the solution delivery architecture to begin.

C : Migration planning should be conducted by the Project Managers using the Implementation and Migration outputs coming out of Phase E. They will use it straightaway in their project plans to narrow down on scope, budget thereon, and time span needed. Best practices from frameworks such as PMP and Prince 2 to arrive at business value envisaged from each project. Project Managers will assign business value and prepare submissions to the IT Governance Board for funding.

The Chief Architect will sit as a member of the Board and advise members with respect to the criticality of the project and its relative importance. Over time the projects will continuously come forward for renewed funding and approval to proceed. The sum of the project plans and roadmaps will serve as the detailed Implementation and Migration Plan.

Once impacts have been resolved, you had to create the views necessary to convey to the stakeholders that their concerns have been addressed with the necessary constraints and guidance developed prior to initiation of solution delivery for it to be successful. You should prove to the stakeholders that when the Architecture Project is consumed by the solution delivery architecture, their requirements have been met and changes to the enterprise will be guided and constrained efficiently.

D : Migration planning should be conducted by the enterprise architecture Team, in particular the domain (Business, Application, Data, Technology, and Security) architects who would look at implementing a series of Transition Architectures using sound project management techniques. The EA Team will then create a prioritized list of activities and place the Building Blocks in an Implementation and Migration Plan and Architecture Roadmap. These deliverables would be circulated around the organization for comments that would be selectively integrated. The circulation would be to the lines of business and the members of the Executive Board so that they would be ready to fund the proposed EA work.

Once impacts have been resolved, you had to create the views necessary to convey to the stakeholders that their concerns have been addressed with the necessary constraints and guidance developed prior to initiation of solution delivery for it to be successful. You noted that the Practitioner's job is to show that a sufficient level of scrutiny led to the deliverables of the Architecture Project for the solution delivery architecture to succeed. You thus identified and secured approval for the resources necessary to begin allocating the budget for the solution delivery architecture to begin.

Proceeding to tackle the question and getting full five marks :

Issues in focus : Integration of the three organizations. Now at the stage of conducting detailed migration planning. Getting this right is critical : Fund, build, support – these are outside EA function.

Aim : An increment approach to rollout the integration program mandated.

To do : to describe :

• How you would conduct migration planning

• What you would be creating that will go for implementing by other teams outside EA

• Who you would involve

• What would be the major deliverable(s)

How should we approach this Scenario based question ?

We need to identify the portion of TOGAF® documentation (available online during Level 2 Exam) so that we can quickly go to that portion and focus only on that. Not more than half a minute to be spent on this search.

10. Phase F: Migration Planning

[1]

Also portions of the answer choices referred to the TOGAF® Series Guide : A Practitioners' Approach to Developing Enterprise Architecture, and the section therein :

A Practitioners' Approach to Developing Enterprise Architecture Following the TOGAF® ADM

[2]

1. https://pubs.opengroup.org/togaf-standard/adm/chap10.html

2. https://pubs.opengroup.org/togaf-standard/adm-practitioners/index.html

9.2.2 Managing the Current Approach towards Implementing the Change

Note the common sentence seen in all ADM Phases : Steps include, not necessary in strict sequential order. In any step related question, the order in which steps appear do not decide any one answer choice to be the best one. However also note that in many cases the order does form some kind of logical flow.

Looking at answer choice A :

Migration planning should be conducted by the Chief Architect through direct reports and shared with the domain architects – Collaborative planning ignored, especially involving other management frameworks. Domain and Segment architects contribute a lot (in Phase E) and this is taken through joint planning exercise towards its development (Implementation) and installation (Migration) planning where PMO, Operations and LOB are involved.

When complete the Plan will be sent to the Architecture Board secretariat for circulation. – Actually should go for approval, not just for circulation and information.

The plan includes : **prioritized list of projects, their approximate cost, and the recommended path.** – Correct point.

Comments from the Board (and their staff) would be incorporated into the plan. – No such steps in TOGAF®. However can be taken as a partly acceptable point.

Plan would include a high-level GANT chart that could be used as the Architecture Roadmap – Correct, but not highly relevant.

The last paragraph, as seen below, is also in line with the portions of the Series Guide referred above, but loses its importance in light of all negative points above. In fact the earlier paragraphs are negating some of the points of the last paragraph.

Once impacts have been resolved, you had to create the views necessary to convey to the stakeholders that their concerns have been addressed with the necessary constraints and guidance developed prior to initiation of solution delivery for it to be successful. You noted that the Practitioner's job is to show that a sufficient level of scrutiny led to the deliverables of the Architecture Project for the solution delivery architecture to succeed. You should prove to the stakeholders that when the Architecture Project is consumed by the solution delivery architecture, their requirements have been met and changes to the Enterprise will be guided and constrained efficiently. You thus identified and secured approval for the resources necessary to begin allocating the budget for the solution delivery architecture to begin.

The approach in this answer choice is incomplete. Phase F emphasizes collaborative planning in close cooperation with the stakeholders within and outside of the organization, and this lacks that approach.

Looking at answer choice B :

All the following are correct points :

Migration Planning by the enterprise architecture Team.

The approach confirmed and coordinated with the corporate management frameworks involved : The Business

---

3. https://pubs.opengroup.org/togaf-standard/adm-practitioners/adm-practitioners_9.html#_Toc95288887

Planning, Portfolio Management, and Operations Management groups should all be involved.

Detailed resource estimates should be created.

Business value identified for all deliverables.

A series of Transition Architectures should be planned along with the priorities.

Once the deliverables have been completed, the architecture development cycle should be completed.

The last paragraph is also in line with the portions of the Series Guide referred above :

Once impacts have been resolved, you had to create the views necessary to convey to the stakeholders that their concerns have been addressed with the necessary constraints and guidance developed prior to initiation of solution delivery for it to be successful. You noted that the Practitioner's job is to show that a sufficient level of scrutiny led to the deliverables of the Architecture Project for the solution delivery architecture to succeed. You should prove to the stakeholders that when the Architecture Project is consumed by the solution delivery architecture, their requirements have been met and changes to the enterprise will be guided and constrained efficiently. You thus identified and secured approval for the resources necessary to begin allocating the budget for the solution delivery architecture to begin.

This appears to be the best answer, unless following answer choices come up with something better. The answer is concise and complete as per Phase F, with an emphasis on building corporate consensus and ensuring that the Transition Architectures are solidly based upon business value.

Looking at answer choice C :

Migration planning should be conducted by the Project Managers using the Implementation and Migration outputs coming out of Phase E. They will use it straightaway in their project plans to narrow down on scope, budget thereon, and time span needed. Best practices from frameworks such as PMP and Prince 2 to arrive at business value envisaged from each project. Project Managers will assign business value and prepare submissions to the IT Governance Board for funding.

Migration planning should be conducted by the Project Managers. – Not so.

Migration planning should be conducted by the Project Managers using the Implementation and Migration outputs coming out of Phase E. – Not correct. EA Team is doing bulk of the work and PMO Team and Project Manages may be involved only as a joint planning exercises after EA finished working on this plan and when is seeking only fine-tuning suggestions.

They will use it straightaway in their project plans to narrow down on scope, budget thereon, and time span needed. Best practices from frameworks such as PMP and Prince 2 to arrive at business value envisaged from each – Somewhat ok, but not for the context of this question scenario. What is stated here is action of PMO after they receive the approved work packages towards the end of Phase F and when the EA team carries out the oversight work in Phase G.

Project Managers will assign business value and prepare submissions to the IT Governance Board. – Not at all so.

The Chief Architect will sit as a member of the Board and advise members. – Not so. Chief Architect is one among the few Board members who direct and decide. But the Chief Architect first plays the role of creating and the finalizing the Architecture and scrutinize it as per Phase F before it goes to the Board.

The sum of the project plans and roadmaps will serve as the detailed Implementation and Migration Plan – partly correct.

The last paragraph, as quoted below, has some relevant points in line with the portions of the Series Guide referred above, but loses its importance in light of all negative points above :

Once impacts have been resolved, you had to create the views necessary to convey to the stakeholders that their concerns have been addressed with the necessary constraints and guidance developed prior to initiation of solution delivery for it to be successful. You should prove to the stakeholders that when the Architecture Project is consumed by the solution delivery architecture, their requirements have been met and changes to the enterprise will be guided and constrained efficiently.

Looking at answer choice D :

Migration planning should be conducted by the enterprise architecture Team. – Correct point. But see the continuation of this point below.

Particularly by the domain (Business, Application, Data, Technology, and Security) architects. – Two possible inaccuracies here : EA conducts the work in Phase F, not domain architects – they may be working on their respective areas in creating SBB in Phase E, but the overall coordination and wok in Phase F is mostly by the Enterprise Architects - Chief Enterprise Architect in collaboration with Segment Architects who are supposed to possess knowledge of multiple domain area in B D A T.; Security is not a discreate domain as per TOGAF®. Still, clubbing it with B D A T seems to be acceptable at the borderline.

Look at implementing a series of Transition Architectures using sound project management techniques. – Outlook here is more towards architecture and less towards project management.

Create a prioritized list of activities and place the Building Blocks in an Implementation and Migration Plan and Architecture Roadmap. – Correct point.

These deliverables would be circulated around the organization for comments that would be selectively integrated. - The circulation would be to the lines of business and the members of the Executive Board so that they would be requested to fund the proposed EA work.

The last paragraph as quoted below has some relevant points in line with the portions of the Series Guide referred above, but loses its importance in light of all negative points above.

Once impacts have been resolved, you had to create the views necessary to convey to the stakeholders that their concerns have been addressed with the necessary constraints and guidance developed prior to initiation of solution delivery for it to be successful. You should prove to the stakeholders that when the Architecture Project is consumed by the solution delivery architecture, their requirements have been met and changes to the enterprise will be guided and constrained efficiently.

This answer choice is a less correct approach, as it is incomplete, missing key steps of Phase F. This also lacks the collaborative planning in close cooperation with the stakeholders within and outside of the organization.

Conclusion and Answer :

Go through all four Observations.

Best answer : B

Second best answer : D : Still nowhere near the best answer

Third best answer : A : Also nowhere near the best answer

Distracter : C

SQ 203

A company that is well established in Store commerce is currently running many stores selling goods needed by domestic customers in many areas of the country. With the trend of buyers shifting to on-line purchases also, they want to extend the same merchandise to be offered through e-Commerce. In order to enable this, they are open to the idea of having dedicated warehouses in certain central areas of the country, having dark stores which are small storge areas in various parts of the respective city apart from using their regular stores also to double up as fulfilment centres.

The CEO has recognized that TOGAF® has played a role in IT areas, evolving over the years right from the time when server hardware and networking equipment were always purchased and installed in data centers with product licenses procured for supporting platform software to present day of Digital Enterprises leveraging Cloud Native trend with Microservices, Data Lakes and many other pieces of the IT puzzle being available purely by subscription basis. The CEO has brought you as the Chief Enterprise Architect, recognizing that even in the changed environment all business functions are needed to deliver an IT capability and this need still exists as the company makes its strides into Digital Transformation.

The CEO has sensitized you that all business functions still require an understanding of the concepts behind the business process, and an approach or methodology to accomplish their associated tasks. You also reciprocated that the TOGAF® version 10 Standard and enterprise architecture are relevant to understand business functions and the tasks that must be completed by people in order to enable the business functions. You have been entrusted with the task of producing a concept document that will prompt the Top Management to give due importance to the initiative ahead in digitizing the newer e-Commerce line of business.

Which of the following options would ideally fit your approach that follows latest TOGAF® standard ?

A : We need to bring in a only a limited and narrow list of drivers in the concept document. Important ones are the drivers that enable the rapid change in technologies that lend themselves to new ways of working, socializing, and entertaining. The enterprise architecture capability and the TOGAF® Standard are not ones supporting Agile software delivery environments. These will not lead to delivering and enhancing digital products and services quicker and easier because they do not provide insight into necessary areas.

The area of such insight to focus on need not include managing technical debt in an reactive way through sprints. These may optionally be directed under appropriate governance. When it comes to managing matured digital products and delivering operational excellence, we need to simplify the complexity in the digital ecosystem using ADM, aiming to establish an EA capability that drives operational excellence in the management of digital products and services. While these are part of Agile Architecture in the digital journey, we need not institutionalize necessary Agile development methods by having them as another framework used in the company.

B : We need to bring in a variety of drivers in the concept document, though one that enable the rapid change in technologies that lend themselves to new ways of working, socializing, and entertaining should get higher weightage among them. The enterprise architecture capability and the TOGAF® Standard is to be seen as one supporting Agile software delivery environments. This in turn will lead to delivering and enhancing digital products and services quicker and easier by providing insight into various areas.

The area of such insight to focus includes managing technical debt in an reactive way through sprints while proactively managing technical debt identifying standards and reusable standard components. These are to be directed under appropriate governance. When it comes to managing matured digital products and delivering operational excellence, we need to simplify the complexity in the digital ecosystem using ADM, aiming to establishing an EA capability that drives operational excellence in the management of digital products and services.

While these are part of Agile Architecture in the digital journey, we also should institutionalize necessary Agile development methods by enabling them as another framework used in the company.

In this connection, Agile delivery must balance the business value of early delivery to market with the future value of leveraging and connecting to other components in the ecosystem that would add value to the product. As a result, a more appropriate approach to developing an Agile backbone may be one that looks at the enterprise, particularly in the Team of Teams and Enduring Enterprise contexts of the DPBoK Standard through the TOGAF® Core Concepts and ADM. Often the quickest delivery involves solutions that are not easily adaptable with other features and difficult to connect to other components in the ecosystem that would add value to the product. It is equally important to consider that for the company to become digital it must improve the digital offerings with products and services that offer additional value not considered by competitors. We should not shy away from experimentation using iterative test-and-learn approaches to identify new digital products, providing the alignment of business objectives to the digital vision, say by applying techniques such as design thinking.

C : We need to bring in a variety of drivers in the concept document. However the least of these are drivers that enable the rapid change in technologies that lend themselves to new ways of working, socializing, and entertaining. The enterprise architecture capability and the TOGAF® Standard is to be seen as one supporting Agile software delivery environments. This in turn will lead to delivering and enhancing digital products and services quicker and easier by providing insight into various areas.

The area of such insight to focus includes managing business debt in an reactive way through sprints while proactively managing this debt identifying standards and reusable standard components. These are to be directed under implementation governance only. When it comes to managing matured digital products and delivering operational excellence, we need to simplify the complexity in the digital ecosystem using ADM, aiming to establishing an EA capability that drives operational excellence in the management of digital products and services.

While these are part of Agile Architecture in the digital journey, we also should institutionalize necessary Agile development methods by enabling them as another framework duly integrated with TOGAF.

In this connection, Agile delivery must balance the business value of early delivery to market with the future value of leveraging and connecting to other components in the ecosystem that would add value to the product. As a result, a more appropriate approach to developing an Agile backbone may be one that looks at the enterprise, particularly in the Team of Teams and Enduring Enterprise contexts of the DPBoK Standard through the TOGAF® Core Concepts and ADM. Often the quickest delivery involves solutions that are not easily adaptable with other features and difficult to connect to other components in the ecosystem that would add value to the product. It is equally important to consider that for the company to become digital it must improve the digital offerings with products and services that offer additional value not considered by competitors. We should not shy away from experimentation using iterative test-and-learn approaches to identify new digital products, providing the alignment of business objectives to the digital vision, say by applying techniques such as design thinking.

D : We need to bring in a variety of drivers in the concept document. However least of these are drivers that enable the rapid change in technologies that lend themselves to new ways of working, socializing, and entertaining. The enterprise architecture capability and the TOGAF® Standard is to be seen as one supporting Agile software delivery environments. This in turn will lead to delivering and enhancing digital products and services quicker and easier by providing insight into various areas.

The area of such insight to focus includes managing technical debt in an reactive way through sprints while proactively managing technical debt identifying standards and reusable standard components. These are to be directed under appropriate governance. When it comes to managing matured digital products and delivering operational excellence, we need to simplify the complexity in the digital ecosystem using ADM, aiming to establishing an EA capability that drives operational excellence in the management of digital products and services.

While these are part of Agile Architecture in the digital journey, we also should institutionalize necessary Agile development methods by enabling them as another framework duly integrated with TOGAF.

In this connection, Agile delivery must balance the business value of early delivery to market with the future value of leveraging and connecting to other components in the ecosystem that would add value to the product. As a result, a more appropriate approach to developing an Agile backbone may be one that looks at the enterprise, particularly in the Team of Teams and Enduring Enterprise contexts of the DPBoK Standard through the TOGAF® Core Concepts and ADM. Often the quickest delivery involves solutions that are not easily adaptable with other features and difficult to connect to other components in the ecosystem that would add value to the product. It is equally important to consider that for the company to become digital it must improve the digital offerings with products and services that offer additional value not considered by competitors. We should not shy away from experimentation using iterative test-and-learn approaches to identify new digital products, providing the alignment of business objectives to the digital vision, say by applying techniques such as design thinking.

Proceeding to tackle the question and getting full five marks :

Issues in focus : Store Commerce to E-Commerce. Digital Transformation.

Aim : Ensuring that all business functions still require an understanding of the concepts behind the business process, and to have an approach or methodology to accomplish their associated tasks.

To do : Best answer among the four alternatives. It has to be in line with the proposed Digital Transformation, as prescribed by the latest version of TOGAF®.

How should we approach this Scenario based question ?

We need to identify the portion of TOGAF® documentation (available online during Level 2 Exam) so that we can quickly go to that portion and focus only on that. Not more than half a minute to be spent on this search.

Points seen above do not make it easy for us to guess the portion, unless some degree of familiarity with the Series Guides is acquired. A reasonable guess will lead us to the Series Guide : Using the TOGAF® Standard in the Digital Enterprise.

The portion to refer therein is :

Using the TOGAF® Standard in the Digital Enterprise
The Open Group

1

2. Why the TOGAF Standard Supports the Digital Enterprise

2.1. Introduction

2

Note that "Team of Teams "is referred to in :

4.4.3. Enterprise Architecture Capabilities and Services: Team of Teams

3

Looking at answer choice A :

Many negative points are spotted :

We need to bring in a only a limited and narrow list of drivers in the concept document.

Important ones are the drivers that enable the rapid change in technologies that lend themselves to new ways of working, socializing, and entertaining.

The enterprise architecture capability and the TOGAF® Standard are not ones supporting Agile software delivery environments.

These will not lead to delivering and enhancing digital products and services quicker and easier because they do not provide insight into necessary areas.

The area of such insight to focus on need not include managing technical debt in an reactive way through sprints.

These may optionally be directed under appropriate governance. – not optionally, but mandatorily.

When it comes to managing matured digital products and delivering operational excellence, we need to simplify the complexity in the digital ecosystem using ADM, aiming to establishing an EA capability that drives operational excellence in the management of digital products and services. – Seems to be the only correct point here.

---

1. https://pubs.opengroup.org/togaf-standard/guides/using-the-togaf-standard-in-the-digital-enterprise/index.html

2. https://pubs.opengroup.org/togaf-standard/guides/using-the-togaf-standard-in-the-digital-enterprise/index.html#_introduction

3. https://pubs.opengroup.org/togaf-standard/guides/using-the-togaf-standard-in-the-digital-enterprise/index.html#_enterprise_architecture_capabilities_and_services_team_of_teams

While these are part of Agile Architecture in the digital journey, we need not institutionalize necessary Agile development methods by having them as another framework used in the company. – Agile development should be a supplementary framework, duly tailored with TOGAF® under these circumstances.

Looking at answer choice B :

We need to bring in a variety of drivers in the concept document, *though one that enable the rapid change in technologies that lend themselves to new ways of working, socializing, and entertaining should get higher weightage among them.* – Later part is not correct. They should not be getting higher weightage.

All other points other than the above one are in line with the Series Guide section.

Looking at answer choice C :

The first paragraph is in line with the Series Guide section.

We need to bring in a variety of drivers in the concept document. However the least of these are drivers that enable the rapid change in technologies that lend themselves to new ways of working, socializing, and entertaining. The enterprise architecture capability and the TOGAF® Standard is to be seen as one supporting Agile software delivery environments. This in turn will lead to delivering and enhancing digital products and services quicker and easier by providing insight into various areas.

However we see conflicting points in the second paragraph :

The area of such insight to focus includes managing business debt in an reactive way through sprints while proactively managing this debt identifying standards and reusable standard components. It is not business debt, but technical debt.

These are to be directed under implementation governance only. – It is not just implementation governance. The Series Guide implies the overall Architectural Governance. It is not aimed just at phase G of ADM. It is covering the entire ADM.

Rest of this are in line with the Series Guide section :

When it comes to managing matured digital products and delivering operational excellence, we need to simplify the complexity in the digital ecosystem using ADM, aiming to establishing an EA capability that drives operational excellence in the management of digital products and services. While these are part of Agile Architecture in the digital journey, we also should institutionalize necessary Agile development methods by enabling them as another framework duly integrated with TOGAF

In this connection, Agile delivery must balance the business value of early delivery to market with the future value of leveraging and connecting to other components in the ecosystem that would add value to the product.

As a result, a more appropriate approach to developing an Agile backbone may be one that looks at the enterprise, particularly in the Team of Teams and Enduring Enterprise contexts of the DPBoK Standard through the TOGAF® Core Concepts and ADM. Often the quickest delivery involves solutions that are not easily adaptable with other features and difficult to connect to other components in the ecosystem that would add value to the product.

It is equally important to consider that for the company to become digital it must improve the digital offerings with products and services that offer additional value not considered by competitors. We should not shy away from experimentation using iterative test-and-learn approaches to identify new digital products, providing the alignment of business objectives to the digital vision, say by applying techniques such as design thinking.

Looking at answer choice D :

Every point here is perfectly in line with the Series Guide section.

Undoubtedly this is the best answer.

Conclusion and Answer :

Go through all four Observations.

Best answer : D

Second best answer : B

Third best answer : C

Distractor : A

SQ 204

ARTI Dimensioning is a multinational that operates production facilities in 29 countries and sells its products in over 120 countries.

A consultancy firm has recommended a realignment that will enhance sharing of product information across business units. The implementation of this strategic realignment will require the development of integrated customer information systems and product information systems.

ARTI has a mature enterprise architecture practice and uses TOGAF® version 10 for the basis of the ARTI Architecture Framework (method and deliverables). The CIO is sponsoring an architecture development program that is going to start. The CIO is concerned about a potential disruptive result to the business of this activity and before proceeding with the architecture development he wanted to evaluate the impacts on the company business. Refer to the scenario above. You are the Lead Architect and you have been asked to recommend an approach to address the concerns raised.

Based on TOGAF®, recommend which of the following is the best answer.

A : A Risk Aversion Assessment should be conducted during the Implementation Governance phase to determine the degree of risk aversion of the proposed business transformation. After sharing the residual level of risk with the company chairman and the residual risk is not accepted, a set of parallel systems will be implemented to mitigate the risks.

B : Your recommendation is to use risk management techniques to assess the risks associated with the proposed business transformation and ensure the existence of business continuity plans. During the Implementation Governance phase you conduct a residual risk assessment to manage risks that cannot be mitigated.

C : During the Architecture Vision phase a risk assessment is conducted to mitigate initial risks and address those in the Architecture Contract signed in the Implementation Governance phase.

D : Your proposal is to utilize a risk management framework during the Implementation Governance phase to verify the risks associated with the proposed transformation of the business. You then share with the concerned stakeholders the residual level on risk before the Architecture Contracts are released.

Proceeding to tackle the question and getting full five marks :

Issues in focus : A scenario question based on risks. Risk is mentioned in more than one ADM Phase. The main treatment of risk management is in Phase E.

The portfolio focus is on development of integrated customer information systems and product information systems.

Aim : To recommend an approach to address the risk concerns raised.

To do : Best description to address the concerns raised.

We do have a chapter on Risk Management

DO NOT PROCEED TILL IT IS OPEN IN A WINDOW IN YOUR SYSTEM

Never forget to open an appropriate documentation section like this, during every reading about and while doing exercises in Level 2 preparation.

For this question, it is :

ADM Techniques
9. Risk Management

[1]

Looking at answer choice A :

Risk Aversion Assessment be **conducted later in the Implementation Governance Phase** to determine the implementation organization's degree of risk aversion with regard to the proposed business transformation. May put in place at that stage a set of parallel systems to mitigate the risks.

Providing name of such an assessment - *Risk Aversion Assessment- this name is not part of TOGAF®.*

Phase G is when implementation (coding and development) starts. *Too late to look into risk possibilities.*

This answer choice *is incorrect and a disaster*. There is no such thing as a Risk Aversion Assessment in TOGAF®. Putting in place a parallel solution would seem excessive and has its own risks.

Looking at answer choice B :

You recommend that techniques be used throughout the program to manage risk including risk monitoring. This will enable you to identify, classify and mitigate the risks associated with the proposed transformation and ensure suitable business continuity plans are in place. In the Implementation Governance phase, you ensure a residual risk assessment is conducted to determine the best way to manage risks that cannot be mitigated.

Risk Management techniques be used throughout ADM, especially risk monitoring.

Will enable you **to identify, classify and mitigate the risks associated with the proposed transformation** and **ensure that suitable business continuity plans** are in place.

Residual risk assessment is conducted later to determine the best way to manage risks that cannot be mitigated. : **Residual risk assessment be conducted later in the Implementation Governance Phase.**

This is **the best answer.** It summarizes the approach recommended in the TOGAF® chapter on Risk Management. It recognizes that risk has to be managed through all phases, and that you need to identify, classify and mitigate risk before starting a transformation. In the Implementation Governance phase, those residual risks should be understood and managed to the extent possible.

Looking at answer choice C :

---

1. https://pubs.opengroup.org/togaf-standard/adm-techniques/chap09.html

During the Architecture Vision phase a risk assessment is conducted to mitigate initial risks and address those in the Architecture Contract signed in the Implementation Governance phase.

Architecture Contracts issued in the Implementation Governance phase *address those initial risks.*

TOGAF® is very clear that risk monitoring actions are given importance in phase E. The initial risk assessment starts in phase A, managing risk takes place in all ADM Phases there onwards, but phase E takes a deeper stock of the risks mitigated and the ones that might arise in subsequent phases. Saying that phase G and the Contracts the will tackle risk is absurd.

Architectural Contracts relate software to developers and users, it has nothing to do with risks being discussed here.

Looking at answer choice D :

Your proposal is to utilize a risk management framework during the Implementation Governance phase to verify the risks associated with the proposed transformation of the business. You then share with the concerned stakeholders the residual level on risk before the Architecture Contracts are released.

Risk management framework is *used in Phase G, the Implementation Governance Phase : Not correct.*

TOGAF® is very clear that risk monitoring actions are given importance in Phase E.

Phase G is when implementation (coding and development) starts. *Too late to look into risk possibilities.*

This answer choice *is less correct* since it does not perform Risk Assessment prior to the Implementation Governance phase. This answer does not address risk monitoring or the management of residual risks.

Conclusion and Answer :

Go through all four Observations.

Best answer : B

Second best : C

Vision Phase gets due mention

Third best : D

Order of Risk related actions is mixed up

Disaster : A

SQ 205

Chiamin Metals is a leading world-wide manufacturer for continuous casting and bottom pouring powders. In addition to mould powders, the company also produces cored wire for secondary metallurgy. Chiamin Metals offers a variety of products and uses a paper-based catalog to promote them.

A new CIO has joined the enterprise and has set up a Team of Enterprise Architects following the TOGAF® practice.

The main challenge is now to offer to Chiamin Metals customers a centralized and reliable entry point for their request via the implementation of a global online portal. This will allow the management of new marketing activities and will enable the new Chiamin Metals' ecommerce service.

You are the Chief Architect and the CIO asked you to present an Architecture Vision to address the above business problem. Identify the best answer according to TOGAF®, version 10.

A : You identify key stakeholders, their concerns, and define the key business requirements to be addressed in the architecture engagement and generate a Stakeholder Map. You evaluate business capabilities and execute a Business Transformation Readiness Assessment. You apply the Business Scenarios technique to create a high-level view of the Baseline and Target Architectures also based on the stakeholder concerns, business capability requirements, scope, constraints, and principles.

B : As requested by the CIO, you focus on the Architecture Vision documentation and apply the Business Scenarios technique to create a high-level view of the Baseline and Target Architectures also based on the stakeholder concerns, business capability requirements, scope, constraints, and principles.

C : You create a high-level view of the Target Architectures and then present them to the CIO.

D : As requested by the CIO you focus on the Architecture Vision and create a detailed view of the Baseline Architectures. This is done for Business, Data, Application and Technology domains and then presented to the CIO using the Architecture Definition Document.

Proceeding to tackle the question and getting full five marks :

Issues in focus :

The main challenge is now to offer to the customers a centralized and reliable entry point for their request via the implementation of a global online portal. This will allow the management of new marketing activities and will enable the new ecommerce service.

To do : To present an Architecture Vision to address the above business problem. Identify the best answer according to TOGAF®.

3. Phase A: Architecture Vision

1

Looking at answer choice A :

You identify key stakeholders, their concerns, and define the key business requirements to be addressed in the architecture engagement and generate a Stakeholder Map. You evaluate business capabilities and execute a Business Transformation Readiness Assessment. You apply the Business Scenarios technique to create a high-level view of the Baseline and Target Architectures also based on the stakeholder concerns, business capability requirements, scope, constraints, and principles.

Every point is relevant. Important points mentioned include Stakeholder Map, Capability Evaluation, Readiness Assessment etc., Also a major (if not every) step of Vision Phase is mentioned here.

Looking at answer choice B :

As requested by the CIO, you **focus on the Architecture Vision documentation and apply the Business Scenarios technique to create a high-level view of the Baseline and Target Architectures also based on the stakeholder concerns, business capability requirements, scope, constraints, and principles.**

All are points relating to steps of Phase A : Architecture Vision. But look for a more detailed answer before voting for this to be the best answer. This may be overtaken by a better answer choice.

Looking at answer choice C :

You create a high-level view of the Target Architectures and then present them to the CIO.

Incomplete and does not describe how this is done.

Looking at answer choice D :

As requested by the CIO you focus on the Architecture Vision and create a detailed view of the Baseline Architectures. **Detailed View (Building Blocks) are prepared in Phases B to D. Not in Phase A: Architecture Vision. The point below becomes redundant by this statement.**

This is done for Business, Data, Application and Technology domains and then presented to the CIO using the Architecture Definition Document.

Conclusion and Answer :

Go through all four Observations.

Best answer : A

All points relevant

Next best answer : B

Relevant points, but not detailed enough

Third best answer : D

See the negative points therein Actually this should be called the second worst answer

Disaster answer : C

Highly incomplete

SQ 206

Hurricane Clothing Company is known for western clothing for men teenagers and children. It has over 100 stores in 10 countries and as of now employees 10,000 people.

It carries a rank of 15 among global clothing retailers. The Design Team in their headquarters at Milano, Italy controls the process steps for preparing the merchandise from its raw material, as also the design and specification and the task of outsourcing of production and all such needs.

This Enterprise is in the process of acquiring three similar fashion chains in order to increase revenue substantially. They are planning to phase in the acquisitions over a period of 3 years.

This Hurricane Clothing Company has a mature enterprise architecture Team. They have been putting TOGAF® into practice for over four years. However it is the first time that this architecture Team is facing the merger of a new entity into the existing enterprise. Main concern of the stakeholders is about their own Security Architecture and its integration with the new acquisitions from different countries and each of which may carry different regulations. Given this situation, the EA Team wants to ensure that the level of importance and scrutiny on the security portion is adequate.

Find the best answer, as per TOGAF® version 10 documentation.

A. Consolidate the companies Information Systems into a single domain in order to reduce the task of security policy development within manageable size. Information objects should be transformed within the information domain in accordance with established rules, conditions and procedures as expressed in the security policy in the domain.

Analyze the minimum security requirement to ensure that the absolute protection will be achieved for the information domain across Communications. Security-Critical functions will be isolated into relatively small modules that are related in well-defined ways. The Operating System will isolate security context from each other using hardware protection features. Untrusted software will use end-system resources only by invoking Security-Critical functions through the separate kernel. Create security association to form as interactive distributed security context. Standardize security management functions, data structures and protocols.

A. Break down the company's Information Systems down into domains to reduce the task of security policy development within manageable size. Information objects should be transferred between two information domains in accordance with established rules, conditions and procedures expressed in the security policy of each information domain.

Analyze the minimum security requirement to ensure that the absolute protection will be achieved for the information domain across Communications. Security-Critical functions will be isolated into relatively small modules that are related in well-defined ways. The Operating System will isolate security context from each other using hardware protection features. Untrusted software will use end-system resources only by invoking Security-Critical functions through the separate kernel. Create security association to form an interactive distributed security context. Standardize security management functions, data structures and protocols.

C : Consolidate the companies Information Systems into a single domain in order to reduce the task of security policy development within manageable size. Hardware should be transferred within the technology domain in accordance with established rules, conditions and procedures expressed in the security and data transfer policies in the domain.

Analyze the minimum security requirement to ensure that the absolute protection will be achieved for the information domain across Communications. Hardware-Critical functions will be isolated into relatively small modules that are related in well-defined ways. The Operating System will isolate security context from each other using hardware protection features. Untrusted software will use end-system resources only by invoking Security-Critical functions through the separate kernel. Create communication associations to form an interactive distributed security context. Standardize security management functions, data structures and protocols.

D : Conduct a risk assessment to classify and identify potential security risks and produce a Risk identification and Mitigation Assessment Worksheet. Initiate an iteration of Requirements Management and based on the updated security requirements, produce and announce new official security policy. Create a Codified Data / Information Asset Ownership and Custody Catalogue.

Conduct an iteration of Phase H to revise Change Management guidelines using the resulting documentation and the Data Classification Policy Catalogue. Gain a complete understanding of the business security requirements; find the pain point of the stakeholders for security considerations; get a clear understanding of what assets need to be protected, from whom they need to be protected, who has authorization to access them and to what level of security they need; document security forensics, perform a threat analysis; assess the impact of new security measures and its side effects; determine "what can go wrong?"

Proceeding to tackle the question and getting full five marks :

Issues in focus :

This Enterprise is in the process of acquiring three similar fashion chains in order to increase revenue substantially. They are planning to phase in the acquisitions over a period of 3 years.

Aim :

Main concern of the stakeholders is about their own Security Architecture and its integration with the new acquisitions from different countries and each of which may carry different regulations.

To do :

Given this situation, the EA Team wants to ensure that the level of importance and scrutiny on the security portion is adequate.

To find the best answer, as per TOGAF® documentation

The answer is evenly spread over Phases C to F. As also some casual reference to a Series Guide.

Architecture Development Method

Integrating Risk and Security within a TOGAF®
Enterprise Architecture
5 Security and Risk Concepts in the TOGAF ADM

Looking at answer choice A :

Consolidate the companies Information Systems into a single domain in order to reduce the task of security policy development within manageable size.- Somewhat acceptable point. Will this consolidation help and is it mentioned in the documentation referred to above ? Not directly, but under 5.3.2 Security Domain Model which mentions :

A security domain represents .... assets that could be described by a .... In other words, the security domain groups the ...... that fall under ..... In addition, the security domain model helps in ....where responsibility is .... : Note that reducing the task of security policy development in provided not by consolidating domains but by breaking them down into many smaller domains. Is this kind of isolation enough ?

Information objects should be transformed within the information domain in accordance with established rules, conditions and procedures as expressed in the security policy in the domain.

Refer to 5.3.1 Security Policy Architecture : The Security Policy Architecture .... contains .... that express .... It assigns .... and a... for security and risk management. It also addresses the ... of operational ... in general with the ... such as ..., ..., ..., and ... security.

Analyze the minimum security requirement to ensure that the absolute protection will be achieved for the information domain across Communications. Security-Critical functions will be isolated into relatively small modules that are related in well-defined ways. The Operating System will isolate security context from each other using hardware protection features. Untrusted software will use end-system resources only by invoking Security-Critical functions through the separate kernel. Create security association to form as interactive distributed security context. Standardize security management functions, data structures and protocols.

Above points appear to be in order. We may not find the exact words in the open book documentation, but it concurs in general with what should be done. But, is this the best answer choice ? We do not yet know. Other answer choices may turn out to be better or worse.

Looking at answer choice B :

Break down the company's Information Systems down into domains to reduce the task of security policy

---

1. https://pubs.opengroup.org/togaf-standard/adm/chap01.html

2. https://pubs.opengroup.org/togaf-standard/integrating-risk-and-security/integrating-risk-and-security_5.html#_Toc95208549

development within manageable size. Information objects should be transferred between two information domains in accordance with established rules, conditions and procedures expressed in the security policy of each information domain.

Analyze the minimum security requirement to ensure that the absolute protection will be achieved for the information domain across Communications. Security-Critical functions will be isolated into relatively small modules that are related in well-defined ways. The Operating System will isolate security context from each other using hardware protection features. Untrusted software will use end-system resources only by invoking Security-Critical functions through the separate kernel. Create security association to form an interactive distributed security context. Standardize security management functions, data structures and protocols.

All are good and acceptable points.

Looking at answer choice C :

Consolidate the companies Information Systems into a single domain in order to reduce the task of security policy development within manageable size.- Somewhat acceptable point. Will this consolidation help and is it mentioned in the documentation referred to above ? Not directly, but under 5.3.2 Security Domain Model which mentions :

A security domain represents .... assets that could be described by a .... In other words, the security domain groups the ...... that fall under ..... In addition, the security domain model helps in ....where responsibility is .... : Note that reducing the task of security policy development here is provided not by consolidating domains but by breaking them down into many smaller domains

Hardware should be transferred within the technology domain in accordance with established rules, conditions and procedures expressed in the security and data transfer policies in the domain. – Not an acceptable point. We do not find such a mention in the documentation.

Analyze the minimum security requirement to ensure that the absolute protection will be achieved for the information domain across Communications. Hardware-Critical functions will be isolated into relatively small modules that are related in well-defined ways. The Operating System will isolate security context from each other using hardware protection features. Untrusted software will use end-system resources only by invoking Security-Critical functions through the separate kernel. Create communication associations to form an interactive distributed security context. Standardize security management functions, data structures and protocols.

– These are acceptable points, except the one on breaking into smaller domains without mention of proper isolation features.

Looking at answer choice D :

Conduct a risk assessment to classify and identify potential security risks and produce a Risk identification and Mitigation Assessment Worksheet. Initiate an iteration of Requirements Management and based on the updated security requirements, produce and announce new official security policy. Create a Codified Data / Information Asset Ownership and Custody Catalogue.

Conduct an iteration of Phase H to revise Change Management guidelines using the resulting documentation and

the Data Classification Policy Catalogue. Gain a complete understanding of the business security requirements; find the pain point of the stakeholders for security considerations; get a clear understanding of what assets need to be protected, from whom they need to be protected, who has authorization to access them and to what level of security they need; document security forensics, perform a threat analysis; assess the impact of new security measures and its side effects; determine "what can go wrong?"

It goes into points which are way out. Also such Artifacts are not seen anywhere in TOGAF®

Conclusion and Answer :

Go through all four Observations.

Best answer : B

Second best : A : Note that reducing the task of security policy development in provided not by consolidating domains but by breaking them down into many smaller domains

Third best : C : Contains references not related to security or those not mentioned in official documentation

Worst Answer : D : It goes into points which are way out. Also such Artifacts are not seen anywhere in TOGAF®

SQ 207

You are serving as the Lead Enterprise Architect at a major supplier in the mechanical component industry. The company is headquartered in a major US state with manufacturing plants across the United States, Brazil, Germany, Japan and South Korea. Each of these plants has been operating its own planning and production scheduling systems, as well as custom developed applications that drive the automated production equipment at each plant.

The company is implementing lean manufacturing principles to minimize waste and improve the efficiency of all of its production operations. During a recent exercise held for internal quality improvement, it was determined that a significant reduction in process waste could be achieved by replacing the current planning and scheduling systems with a common Enterprise Resource Planning (ERP) system located in the central data center.

This central system would provide support to each of the plants replacing the functionality in the existing systems. It would also eliminate the need for full data centers at each of the plant facilities. A reduced number of IT staff could support the remaining applications. In some cases, a third-party contractor could provide those staff.

The enterprise architecture department has been operating for several years and has mature, well developed architecture governance and development processes that are strongly based on TOGAF®.

At a recent meeting, the Architecture Board approved a Request for Architecture Work sponsored by the Chief Engineer of Global Manufacturing Operations. The request covered the initial architectural investigations and the development of a comprehensive architecture to plan the transformation.

A : The Team should develop Baseline and Target Architectures for each of the manufacturing plants, ensuring that the views corresponding to selected viewpoints address key concerns of the stakeholders. A consolidated gap analysis between the architectures will then be used to validate the approach, and determine the capability increments needed to achieve the target state.

B: The Team should exercise due diligence and carefully research vendor literature and conduct a series of briefings with vendors that are on the current approved supplier list. Based on the findings from the research, the Team should define a preliminary Architecture Vision. The Team should then use that model to build consensus among the key stakeholders.

C: The Team should use stakeholder analysis to understand who has concerns about the initiative. The Team should then hold a series of interviews at each of the manufacturing plants using the business scenario technique. This will then enable them to identify and document the key high-level stakeholder requirements for the architecture.

D: The Team should conduct a pilot project that will enable vendors on the short list to demonstrate potential solutions that will address the concerns of the stakeholders. Based on the findings of that pilot project, a complete set of solutions will be developed that will drive the evolution of the architecture.

Proceeding to tackle the question and getting full five marks :

Where are we :

Request for Architecture Work approved. Vision Phase started. Note that the scenarios is about concerns and the way to proceed to address them.

In short, it is about Stakeholder Management.

What to refer :

The TOGAF® Standard

ADM Techniques

1

3. Stakeholder Management

2

3. Stakeholder Management[3]

Looking at answer choice A :

The Team should develop Baseline and Target Architectures for each of the manufacturing plants, ensuring that the views corresponding to selected viewpoints address key concerns of the stakeholders. A consolidated gap analysis between the architectures will then be used to validate the approach, and determine the capability increments needed to achieve the target state.

Does any of this happen in Phase A ? Not at all. Developing Baseline and Target are part of Phase B to D. Consolidated Gap happens in Phase E. The Scenario of this question is purely is on Phase A and Stakeholder Engagement begins at that stage.

Looking at answer choice B :

The Team should exercise due diligence and carefully research vendor literature and conduct a series of briefings with vendors that are on the current approved supplier list. Based on the findings from the research, the Team should define a preliminary Architecture Vision. The Team should then use that model to build consensus among the key stakeholders.

There is nothing like a 'preliminary Architecture vision'.

Nevertheless "build consensus among the key stakeholders" is mentioned. This happens in Phase B to D. **Stakeholders are identified as per a Matrix in Phase A** and only a high level aspirational view, known as Vision Document is formed.

Looking at answer choice C :

---

1. https://pubs.opengroup.org/togaf-standard/adm-techniques/index.html

2. https://pubs.opengroup.org/togaf-standard/adm-techniques/chap03.html

3. **https://pubs.opengroup.org/togaf-standard/adm-techniques/chap03.html**

The Team should use stakeholder analysis to understand who has concerns about the initiative. The Team should then hold a series of interviews at each of the manufacturing plants using the business scenario technique. This will then enable them to identify and document the key high-level stakeholder requirements for the architecture.

Every point here is all about the scenario need : "concern about the security and reliability of diving their planning and production scheduling from a remote centralized system."

Looking at answer choice D :

The Team should conduct a pilot project that will enable vendors on the short list to demonstrate potential solutions that will address the concerns of the stakeholders. Based on the findings of that pilot project, a complete set of solutions will be developed that will drive the evolution of the architecture.

Many Level 2 Exam questions may mention a pilot project. *But we do not see this phrase anywhere in TOGAF® documentation.*

Vendor and vendor brand related activities come in only in something like Phase E partly and mostly in Phase F. These **do not connect with the task of 'addressing the Stakeholder concerns'.**

Conclusion and Answer :

Go through all four Observations.

Best answer : C :

Because it focusses on Stakeholder engagement

Not correct answers : (Ranking among them here is not a very good idea. You can try purely as an academic exercises, if needed)

A : Not something done in Vision Phase. These happen in Phases B to D. But the scenario is focussed on Phase A

B : Very generic and non-specific answer

D : Pilot project is never mentioned in TOGAF® anywhere

SQ 208

UTrack Transports is a strong UK logistics company. The head of the strategic marketing division engaged the Principal Architect issuing a Request for architectural work to design an enhancement of the current Enterprise Data Warehouse system.

An enhancement is needed to support the change in the business model; UTrack wants to leverage on customer data collected during business as usual activities and anonymize them to offer marketing agencies a fresh and accessible source of analytics data. This is expected to increase the company revenues.

TOGAF® is the architectural framework in use. The Principal Architect has decided to ask you as Business Intelligence Subject Matter Expert to design the Data Architecture. The Chief Architect shared with you the Architecture Definition Document worked upon so far, including the Business Architecture design. You now need to choose the artifacts you want to produce as part of the Data Architecture design. Identify the best answer according to TOGAF®.

A : You first list the data used across the enterprise using a Data Entity/Data Component Catalog, including data entities and also the data components where data entities are stored. You then classify what the data source are and the relationship with the data entities via a System/Data Matrix. You finally identify common data requirements using a Data Lifecycle Diagram.

B : You first list the data used across the enterprise using a Data Entity/Data Component Matrix, including data entities and also the data components where data entities are stored. You then classify what the data source are and the relationship with the data entities via a Role/System Catalog. You finally identify common data requirements using a Data Use Case Diagram.

C : You first list the data used across the enterprise using a Data Entity/Data Component Catalog, including data entities and also the data components where data entities are stored. You then classify what the data source are and the relationship with the data entities via a System/Data Matrix.

D : You first list the data used across the enterprise using a Data Entity/Data Component Catalog, including data entities and also the data components where data entities are stored. You then assign ownership of data entities to the organization via a System/Data Matrix.

Proceeding to tackle the question and getting full five marks :

Request for Architecture Work – Issued. Vision Phase, though not specifically mentioned, has been gone through.

To design the Data Architecture as an enhancement of the current Enterprise Data Warehouse system.

To refer :

6. Phase C: Information Systems Architectures — Data Architecture

[1]

Also :

3.6.4 Phase C: Data Architecture

Which is part of

Architecture Content
3. Architectural Artifacts

[2]

Go through all Artifacts mentioned, especially those relating to Data Architecture.

Looking at answer choice A :

You first list the data used across the enterprise using a Data Entity/Data Component Catalog, including data entities and also the data components where data entities are stored. You then classify what the data source are and the relationship with the data entities via a System/Data Matrix. You finally identify common data requirements using a Data Lifecycle Diagram.

Data Entity/Data Component Matrix : **Relevant** to identify and maintain a list of all the data use across the enterprise, including data entities and also the data components where data entities are stored.

System/Data Matrix : **Relevant** to depict the relationship between applications (i.e., application components) and the data entities that are accessed and updated by them.

You finally identify common data requirements using a Data Lifecycle Diagram : **Highly relevant point, for a Data Warehouse Architecture.**

Looking at answer choice B :

You first list the data used across the enterprise using a Data Entity/Data Component Matrix, including data entities and also the data components where data entities are stored. You then classify what the data source are and the relationship with the data entities via a Role/System Catalog. You finally identify common data requirements using a Data Use Case Diagram.

Data Entity/Data Component Matrix : **Relevant** to identify and maintain a list of all the data use across the enterprise,

---

including data entities and also the data components where data entities are stored.

Role/System Catalog : *Not Relevant* : It depicts the relationship between applications and the business roles that use them within the enterprise.

Data Use Case Diagram : **Can show the scenarios** which relate to Data and the way Data Visualization is done from the Data Warehouse. This diagram can be taken as a variation of the Application Use Case diagram mentioned under the artifact suggestion of Application Architecture.

Looking at answer choice C :

You first list the data used across the enterprise using a Data Entity/Data Component Catalog, including data entities and also the data components where data entities are stored. You then classify what the data source are and the relationship with the data entities via a System/Data Matrix.

Data Entity/Data Component Matrix : **Relevant**

System/Data Matrix : **Relevant** to depict the relationship between applications (i.e., application components) and the data entities that are accessed and updated by them.

Looking at answer choice D :

You first list the data used across the enterprise using a Data Entity/Data Component Catalog, including data entities and also the data components where data entities are stored. You then assign ownership of data entities to the organization via a System/Data Matrix.

Data Entity/Data Component Matrix : **Relevant.**

System/Data Matrix : **Relevant,** but more useful for relationship match than ownership claim.

Conclusion and Answer :

Go through all four Observations.

Best answer : A

Because Artifact – Building Blocks are chosen appropriately

C is second best.

Has couple of relevant points

D is third best.

Has one clearly relevant points and another generally acceptable point

B is the worst answer

Has an irrelevant point

SQ 209

Carter Woods, a global furniture firm, wants to improve the efficiency of its sales force by replacing their legacy configuration and ordering systems based on manual and paper based processes with an online ordering platform.

Carter Woods uses the Architecture Development Method from TOGAF®. The CIO sponsored this activity and the Baseline Architecture was defined on the initial iteration defining: approach, scope and architectural vision including a set of architecture principles related to the Data domain :

- Data is an asset.

- Data is shared.

- Data is accessible.

A set of aspects to clarify arose from the business analysis from the assumption to replace the legacy systems with an online centralized one. These main concerns are :

· To identify the changes to existing business processes.

· To identify the data entities that can be shared among the sales agents.

· To clarify how to keep the data secured.

· To identify the list of non-sales application to be integrated with the sales applications.

You, as Lead Enterprise Architect, need to identify the most appropriate architecture viewpoints to address the concerns above mentioned. Choose one of the following answers :

A : Depict the Business Architecture using a Role catalog and a process/Event/Control/Product catalog. Depict the Data Architecture using a System/Data matrix, a Data Entity/Data Component catalog and Data Security diagram. Depict the Application Architecture using an Interface catalog. Define the Technology Architecture via a Network Computing/Hardware diagram.

B : Depict the Business Architecture using a Business Event diagram and a Location catalog. Depict the Data Architecture using a Data Lifecycle diagram and a Data Migration diagram as also a Role Data catalog. Depict the Application Architecture using a Software Engineering diagram and Data over Application Matrix. Depict the Technology Architecture using a Communications Engineering diagram.

C : Depict the Business Architecture using a Business Footprint diagram and a Location catalog. Depict the Data Architecture using a Data Migration diagram, System/Data matrix and Data Lifecycle diagram. Depict the Application Architecture using an Application Communication diagram. Depict the Technology Architecture using a Network Computing/Hardware diagram.

D : Depict the Business Architecture using a Role catalog and Location catalog. Depict the Data Architecture using a System/Data matrix, Data Entity/Business Function matrix and Data Security diagram. Depict the Application Architecture using an Application Interaction matrix. Define the Technology Architecture via a Network Computing/ Hardware diagram.

Proceeding to tackle the question and getting full five marks :

What to refer :

Architecture Content
3. Architectural Artifacts

[1]

Go through the artifact list mentioned in each answer choice, in the context of the Principles that are to be adhered to and the concerns to be addressed.

Looking at answer choice A :

Depict the Business Architecture using a Role catalog and also a Process/Event/Control/Product catalog. Depict the Data Architecture using a System/Data matrix, a Data Entity/Data Component catalog and Data Security diagram. Depict the Application Architecture using an Interface catalog. Define the Technology Architecture via a Network Computing/Hardware diagram.

Role catalog : To provide a listing of all authorization levels or zones within the Enterprise : **For Principle - Data is accessible. Towards the concern : To clarify how to keep the data secured.**

Process/Event/Control/Product catalog : To provide a hierarchy of processes, events that trigger processes, outputs from processes, and controls applied to the execution of processes. **For Principle - Data is shared. Towards the concern : To identify the changes to existing business processes.**

(Application) System/Data matrix : Application/Data Matrix to depict the relationship between applications (i.e., application components) and the data entities that are accessed and updated by them. **For Principle - Data is an asset. Towards the concern : To identify the list of non-sales application to be integrated with the sales applications and to identify the data entities that can be shared among the sales agents.**

Data Security diagram : To show which data is accessed by which roles, organization units, and applications. **For Principle - Data is accessible. Towards the concern : To clarify how to keep the data secured.**

Interface Catalog : It demarcates the scope over which the interface and the functionalities exposed by it operates. Thus it serves as a documentation of the interface between one (service) application and another. Thus it serves the purpose of enabling the overall dependencies between (services) applications. Very useful during early part of architecture work in clarifying the scope of such (services) applications. **Proper documentation of the interfaces can be used to satisfy two Principles : Data is shared; Data is accessible. It addresses all four concerns.**

Networked Computing/Hardware Diagram : It shows the logical view of how various logical application

---

components are deployed. It reveals the topology of the distributed network computing environment. **It is the way to distribute properly, against the Principle of - Data is an asset. It can partially address the concern : To identify the data entities that can be shared among the sales agents**

Looking at answer choice B :

Depict the Business Architecture using a Business Event diagram and a Location catalog. Depict the Data Architecture using a Data Lifecycle diagram and a Data Migration diagram as also a Role Data catalog. Depict the Application Architecture using a Software Engineering diagram and Data over Application Matrix. Depict the Technology Architecture using a Communications Engineering diagram.

Role Data catalog : No such catalog in artifact list of TOGAF

Data over Application Matrix : No such matrix in artifact list of TOGAF

Also, look at the following :

Business Event diagram

Location catalog.

Data Lifecycle diagram

System/Data matrix

Data Migration diagram

Software Engineering diagram

Communications Engineering diagram

Go through the link given above and see if any of these are relevant to the scenario of the question. *You may not find much.*

Looking at answer choice C :

Depict the Business Architecture using a Business Footprint diagram, Product Lifecycle diagram and a Location catalog. Depict the Data Architecture using a Data Migration diagram, System/Data matrix and Data Lifecycle diagram. Depict the Application Architecture using an Application Communication diagram. Depict the Technology Architecture using a Network Computing/Hardware diagram and Platform Decomposition Diagram

Business Footprint diagram

Product Lifecycle diagram

Location catalog

Data Migration diagram

Application Communication diagram

Network Computing/Hardware diagram

Platform Decomposition Diagram

Go through the link given above and see if any of these are relevant to the scenario of the question. *You may not find much.*

System/Data matrix : See discussion in a choice above. **This artifact is relevant.**

Looking at answer choice D :

Depict the Business Architecture using a Role catalog and Business Event diagram as also a Value Stream Map. Depict the Data Architecture using a System/Data matrix, Data Entity/Business Function matrix and Data Security diagram. Depict the Application Architecture using an Application Interaction matrix. Define the Technology Architecture via a Network Computing/Hardware diagram and Platform Decomposition Diagram.

Role catalog

System/Data matrix

Data Security diagram

All three above are relevant as per discussion seen in another answer choice above.

Entity/Business Function matrix to depict the relationship between data entities and business functions within the enterprise.

Can be considered somewhat relevant to the scenario of the question.

Business Event diagram

Value Stream Map.

Application Interaction matrix

Network Computing/Hardware diagram

Platform Decomposition Diagram

Go through the link given above and see if any of these are relevant to the scenario of the question. *You may not find much.*

Conclusion and Answer :

Go through all four Observations.

Best answer : A

Discussion above for each artifact against the Principles and concern justifies this

Second best answer : D

Obviously more points that agree

Third best answer : C

At least one point in line with the scenario

Worst answer : B

You can see how it disagrees on every count

SQ 210

McKinley Rockets is an enterprise that employs 20,000 people in five countries: UK, Italy, France, Spain and the Netherlands and its mission is to guarantee access to space offering space transportation, launch and management of satellite systems at low cost.

A TOGAF® based mature enterprise architecture program is already established within the enterprise. McKinley Rockets strategy is to leverage in the USA shortage of satellite launches availability - that NASA created because of the Shuttle program shutdown - by acquiring an important American space agency. This will ultimately allow McKinley Rockets to offer its services to the US market.

The new acquired company NovaSpace is very successful but with outdated satellite monitoring systems. The CIO is sponsoring an activity to extend the McKinley Rockets' satellite monitoring applications to include the NovaSpace's satellites flock.

Architecture Board decided to approve the vision, provided that the Design Definition Document is presented for review at phase D conclusion.

The Chief Architect asked you as Lead Integration Architect to use TOGAF® to recommend the best approach to design the Full Architecture and present it to the Architecture Board.

Identify the best answer accordingly to the TOGAF® version 10 guidelines.

A : You start with the Business Architecture and then address Technology, Application and Data domains, in that order.

For every domain you select the relevant reference models, viewpoints, and tools.

You develop a Target and Baseline Architecture Descriptions. Then perform Gap Analysis, resolve impacts across the Architecture Landscape and update the roadmap. Finally update the Architecture Definition Document.

B : You start with the Business Architecture and then address Data, Application and Technology domains.

You then Confirm management framework interactions for the Implementation and Migration Plan, Prioritize the migration projects through the conduct of a cost/benefit assessment and risk validation. Then perform Gap Analysis and update the Architecture Definition Document.

C : You start with the Business Architecture and then address Data, Application and Technology domains. For every domain you select the relevant reference models, viewpoints, and tools. You develop a Baseline and Target Architecture. Then perform Gap Analysis, assess the roadmap impacts and finally update the Architecture Definition Document.

D : You start with the Business Architecture and then address Data, Application and Technology domains. For every domain you develop a Baseline and Target Architecture. Then perform Gap Analysis and update the Architecture Definition Document.

Proceeding to tackle the question and getting full five marks :

Scenario is about a larger approach to design the Full Architecture and present it to the Architecture Board. This means the focus is on B D A T segments which fall under phases B to phase D.

To do

Identify the best answer (which is in line withs steps of phase B to D)

What to refer :

Note that steps of phase B to phase D have lot of similarity. We can refer to any one phase and extend the ideas to other phases.

- X.3.1 Select Reference Models, Viewpoints, and Tools
- X. 3.2 Develop Baseline Architecture Description
- X.3.3 Develop Target Architecture Description
- X.3.4 Perform Gap Analysis
- X.3.5 Define Candidate Roadmap Components
- X.3.6 Resolve Impacts Across the Architecture Landscape
- X.3.7 Conduct Formal Stakeholder Review
- X.3.8 Finalize the XXX Architecture
- X.3.9 Create the Architecture Definition Document

Looking at answer choice A :

You **start with the Business Architecture** *and then address Technology, Application and Data domains, in that order. – The order should be such that Technology Architecture comes last.*

For every domain you select the relevant reference models, viewpoints, and tools. – Generally ok. Domain here refers to the four Segments of B D A T.

You **develop a Target and Baseline Architecture Descriptions.** Then **perform Gap Analysis, resolve impacts across the Architecture Landscape and update the roadmap.** Finally **update the Architecture Definition Document.** – Generally ok.

Looking at answer choice B :

You start with the Business Architecture and then address Data, Application and Technology domains. – Generally ok.

You then *Confirm management framework interactions for the Implementation and Migration Plan, Prioritize the migration projects through the conduct of a cost/benefit assessment and risk validation. All steps of Phase F. Not suiting the need of this scenario.*

Then perform **Gap Analysis and update the Architecture Definition Document.** – Generally ok, *but none of these occur after Phase F. The 'then' is misleading.*

Looking at answer choice C :

You start with the Business Architecture and then address Data, Application and Technology domains. For every domain you select the relevant reference models, viewpoints, and tools. You develop a Baseline and Target Architecture. Then perform Gap Analysis, assess the roadmap impacts and finally update the Architecture Definition Document.

Every point and its order are fine. Most of the steps are included (though resolving impacts through peer analysis and Stakeholder Review are missing).

Nevertheless, this is best among the answer choices.

Note the 'not suitable' points in the discussion above.

Looking at answer choice D :

You start with the Business Architecture and then address Data, Application and Technology domains. For every domain you develop a Baseline and Target Architecture. Then perform Gap Analysis and update the Architecture Definition Document. – Generally ok. *But compare with the steps of B D A T related Phases, and you will notice that a few points are missing.*

Conclusion and Answer :

Go through all four Observations.

Best answer : C

See discussion above

Second best answer : D

Few points missed out

Third best answer : A

At least one incorrect point

Worst answer : B

Note the 'not suitable' points in the discussion above

You are serving as the Chief Architect for a large, global commodities trading company which has been growing rapidly through a series of acquisitions.

Each business is performing well in its markets. However, the lack of integration between headquarters and the business units has increasingly caused problems in the handling of customer and financial information. The inability to share information across businesses has resulted in lost opportunities to "leverage the synergies" that had been intended when the businesses were acquired. At present, each business unit maintains its own applications. Despite an earlier initiative to install a common application to manage customer, products, supplier, and inventory information, each business unit has different ways of defining each of these core elements and has customized the common application to the point where the ability to exchange information is difficult, costly, and error-prone.

As a result, the company has made the decision to introduce a single enterprise-wide application to consolidate information from several applications that exist across the lines of business. The application will be used by all business units and accessed by suppliers through well-defined interfaces.

The Corporate Board is concerned that the new application must be able to manage and safeguard confidential customer information in a secure manner that meets or exceeds the legal requirements of the countries in which the company operates. This will be an increasingly important capability as the company expands its online services in cooperation with its trading partners.

The CIO has formed an enterprise architecture department, and one of the primary goals in its charter is to coordinate efforts between the implementation Team and the business unit personnel who will be involved in the migration process.

The CIO has also formed a cross-functional Architecture Board to oversee and govern the architecture. The company has an existing Team of security architects.

TOGAF® has been selected for use for the enterprise architecture program. The CIO has endorsed this choice with the full support of top management.

Based on TOGAF®, which of the following is the best answer ?

A : You start by clarifying the intent that the Board has for raising these concerns. This enables you to understand the implications of the concern in terms of regulatory requirements and the potential impact on current business goals and objectives. You propose that a security architect or security architecture Team be allocated to develop a comprehensive security architecture and that this be considered an additional domain architecture.

B : You evaluate the implications of the Board's concerns by examining the security and regulatory impacts on business goals, business drivers and objectives. Based on your understanding, you then update the current security policy to include an emphasis on the concerns. You define architecture principles to form constraints on the architecture work to be undertaken in the project. You then allocate a security architect to ensure that security considerations are included in the architecture planning for all domains.

C : You identify and document the security and regulatory requirements for the application and the data being collected. You ensure that written policies are put in place to address the requirements, and that they are communicated across the organization, together with appropriate training for key employees. You identify constraints on the architecture and communicate those to the architecture Team. You establish an agreement with the security architects defining their role within the ongoing architecture project.

D : You evaluate the implications of the concerns raised by the Corporate Board in terms of regulatory requirements and their impact on business goals and objectives. Based on this understanding, you then issue a Request for Architecture Work to commence an architecture development project to develop a solution that will address the concerns. You allocate a security architect to oversee the implementation of the new application that is being developed.

Proceeding to tackle the question and getting full five marks :

What to refer :

2. Preliminary Phase

1

Looking at answer choice A :

You start by clarifying **the intent that the Board has for raising these concerns.** This enables you to **understand the implications** of the concern in terms of regulatory requirements and the potential impact on current business goals and objectives.

You propose that a security architect or security architecture Team be allocated to develop a comprehensive security architecture and that this be considered an additional domain architecture.

EA Team should take the lead and guide the Security Team. This point is not proper here.

Looking at answer choice B :

You evaluate the implications of the Board's concerns by **examining the security and regulatory impacts on business goals, business drivers and objectives**. Based on your understanding, you then **update the current security policy to include an emphasis on the concerns.**

Policy or even Principles update is a good point.

You **define architecture principles** to form constraints on the architecture work to be undertaken in the project.

One more step in right direction.

You then *allocate a security architect* to ensure that security considerations are included in the architecture planning

1. https://pubs.opengroup.org/togaf-standard/adm/chap02.html

for all domains.

EA Team should take the lead and guide the Security Team. This point is not proper here.

Looking at answer choice C :

You identify and document the **security and regulatory requirements for the application and the data being collected.**

Good beginning and data related security and regulatory concern are identified.

You ensure that **written policies are put in place** to address the requirements, and that they are **communicated across the organization,** together with appropriate training for key employees.

Three great points : Policy and Principles formulation; communicating them; arranging for training upfront.

You identify constraints on the architecture and communicate those to the architecture Team.

EA plays its right role in this Preliminary Phase.

You establish an agreement with the security architects defining their role within the ongoing architecture project.

This is something about the Request for Architecture work as also Statement of Architecture Work.

Every point is perfect.

Looking at answer choice D :

You **evaluate the implications of the concerns raised** by the Corporate Board in terms of regulatory requirements and their impact on business goals and objectives.

Good point.

Based on this understanding, you then issue a Request for Architecture Work to commence an architecture development project to develop a solution that will address the concerns.

Good point, but *involving Security Architect here could have been better.*

You allocate a security architect to oversee the implementation of the new application that is being developed.

Good Point.

Conclusion and Answer :

Go through all four Observations.

Best answer : C

Discussion above will convince you why

Second best answer : D

Came close to being the best answer

Third best answer : B

Some good points, but one incorrect mark

Worst answer : A

Answering here could not come close to the Scenario need, except in one point

SQ 212

Eight Twelve has retail outlets throughout North America. An enterprise architecture practice already exists in Eight Twelve. Now the CEO and CIO decide that they want to use TOGAF® to re-architect their enterprise architecture to cater to the changing strategies of Eight Twelve to better respond to the changes in the economic and technology environments.

Some of the key issues which need to be addressed in this re-architecting work are :

1. Since Eight Twelve's retail chain operate 24 hours a day and are expanding to South America and Europe, the retail chain business ecosystem should be able to withstand any unforeseen disruptions which might affect the chain's day to day operations. This is highly critical to ensure high levels of customer satisfaction and thus maintaining and enhancing Eight Twelve's revenue chain.
2. Dependency between the application components, which are the nerve centers to Eight Twelve's sophisticated range of services both external and internal, and the application platform and technology infrastructure should be minimal. This would facilitate scalability and ease of enhancement of the service offerings.
3. Eight Twelve uses the ARTS Data Model and the quality of data is of utmost importance for its operation.
4. Users of the Enterprise Information ecosystem should have an environment which is able to cater to their needs without any undue delays.

Which one of the following set of Architecture Principles do you feel is the most appropriate for these guidelines stated above for the TOGAF® architecting work which Eight Twelve is embarking on ?

A.

a) Maximize Benefit to the Enterprise

b) Data Trustee

c) Service Orientation

d) Responsive Change Management

B.

a) Business Continuity

b) Data is an Asset

c) Data is Shared

d) Requirements Based Change

C.

a) Maximize Benefit to the Enterprise

b) Data is an Asset

c) Data is Shared

d) Requirements Based Change

D.

a) Business Continuity

b) Data Trustee

c) Technology Independence

d) Responsive Change Management

Proceeding to tackle the question and getting full five marks :

What to refer :

ADM Techniques
2. Architecture Principles

[1]

Issues in Re-architecting are :

P. High levels of customer satisfaction

Q. Dependency between the application components

R. Quality of data (they are using an Industry specific Architecture, ARTS)

S. Cater to needs without any undue delays

Looking at answer choice A :

a) Maximize Benefit to the Enterprise

b) Data Trustee : **Matches Issue R)**

c) Service Orientation : **Matches Issue Q)**

d) Responsive Change Management

Looking at answer choice B :

---

1. https://pubs.opengroup.org/togaf-standard/adm-techniques/chap02.html

a) Business Continuity : **Matches Issue S)**

b) Data is an Asset

c) Data is Shared

d) Requirements Based Change : **Matches Issue P)**

Looking at answer choice C :

a) Maximize Benefit to the Enterprise

b) Data is an Asset

c) Data is Shared

d) Requirements Based Change : **Matches Issue P)**

Looking at answer choice D :

a) Business Continuity : **Matches Issue S)**

b) Data Trustee : **Matches Issue R)**

c) Technology Independence : **Matches Issue Q)**

d) Responsive Change Management : **Matches Issue P)**

Conclusion and Answer :

Go through all four Observations.

Best answer : D

Most matches

Second best answer : A or could be B

Two matches each

Worst answer : C

One match

SQ 213

Marona Inc is a Fortune 500 Enterprise in the retail industry with retail store components manufacturing units and marketing outlets spanning the globe and having an annual turnover of $ 20 billion with more than 100,000 employees worldwide.

The CEO, CIO and the stakeholders of the ongoing EA projects are concerned about rising costs and as one measure want to do an investigation into the operational aspects of the realized enterprise architecture using TOGAF®.

The CIO approaches you as the Lead Enterprise Architect to carry out this exercise. The stakeholder had voiced to him the following concerns :

They want to analyze the roles of the top management for each revenue earning service. Moreover, many of the HR related critical Search application components have become extremely slow. This needs to be diagnosed and rectified. Moreover there is no proper tracking of revenue from retail store component products over time.

There has also been a lot of unauthorized or unwanted access to many of the critical information.

Hence the mode of access needs to be strengthened and made much more secure. Another additional concern is the new launches and the progress of each of the launches over time.

Determine which of the following set of artifacts are most appropriate to analyze and view in order to address this concern of the stakeholders.

A.

(i) System/Functions Matrix

(ii) Actor/Role Matrix

(iii) Data Entity/Business Function Matrix

(iv) Technology Portfolio Catalog

(v) Data Security Diagram

B.

(i) Goal/Objective/Service Diagram

(ii) Contract Measure Catalog

(iii) Data Dissemination Diagram

(iv) Application Communication Diagram

(v) Data Life Cycle Diagram

C.

(i) Location Catalog

(ii) Service/Function Catalog

(iii) Data Entity/Business Function Matrix

(iv) Application Communication Diagram

D.

(i) Actor/Role Matrix

(ii) System/Technology Matrix

(iii) Goal/Objective/Service Diagram

(iv) Product Life Cycle Diagram

(v) Data Security Diagram

Proceeding to tackle the question and getting full five marks :

What to refer :

Architecture Content
3. Architectural Artifacts

[1]

Concerns and Issues : Rising costs - operational aspects needs relook

Need to :

P. Analyze roles of the top management for each revenue earning service

Q. Diagnose and rectify (HR related) application for speed

R. Unauthorized or unwanted access to critical information

S. Monitoring timely progress of new launches

T. Proper tracking of revenue from retail store component products over time

Looking at answer choice A :

(i) System/Functions Matrix[2] : (Application/Function Matrix) : to depict the relationship between applications and business functions within the enterprise

---

1. https://pubs.opengroup.org/togaf-standard/architecture-content/chap03.html

2. https://pubs.opengroup.org/togaf-standard/architecture-content/chap03.html#tag_03_06_05_05

(ii) Actor/Role Matrix[3] : To show which actors perform which roles, supporting definition of security and skills requirements. : **Matches P)**

(iii) Data Entity/Business Function Matrix[4] : To depict the relationship between data entities and business functions within the enterprise

(iv) Technology Portfolio Catalog[5] : To identify and maintain a list of all the technology in use across the enterprise, including hardware, infrastructure software, and application software

(v) Data Security Diagram[6] : Shows which data is accessed by which roles, organization units, and applications : **Matches R)**

Looking at answer choice B :

(i) Goal/Objective/Service Diagram[7] : To define the ways in which a business service contributes to the achievement of a business vision or strategy : **Matches T)**

(ii) Contract Measure Catalog[8] : Provides a listing of all agreed service contracts and the measures attached to those contracts

(iii) Data Dissemination Diagram[9] : To show the relationship between data entity, business service, and application components

(iv) Application Communication Diagram[10] : To depict all models and mappings related to communication between applications in the metamodel entity

(v) Data Life Cycle Diagram[11] : Helps in managing business data throughout its lifecycle from conception until disposal within the constraints of the business process

Looking at answer choice C :

(i) Location Catalog[12] : Provides a listing of all locations where an enterprise carries out business operations or houses architecturally relevant assets, such as data centers or end-user computing equipment

(ii) Service/Function Catalog[13] : To provide a functional decomposition in a form that can be filtered, reported on, and queried, as a supplement to graphical Functional Decomposition diagrams

(iii) Data Entity/Business Function Matrix[14] : As discussed above, to depict the relationship between data entities and

3. https://pubs.opengroup.org/togaf-standard/architecture-content/chap03.html#tag_03_06_03_13

4. https://pubs.opengroup.org/togaf-standard/architecture-content/chap03.html#tag_03_06_04_02

5. https://pubs.opengroup.org/togaf-standard/architecture-content/chap03.html#tag_03_06_06_02

6. https://pubs.opengroup.org/togaf-standard/architecture-content/chap03.html#tag_03_06_04_07

7. https://pubs.opengroup.org/togaf-standard/architecture-content/chap03.html#tag_03_06_03_21

8. https://pubs.opengroup.org/togaf-standard/architecture-content/chap03.html#tag_03_06_03_07

9. https://pubs.opengroup.org/togaf-standard/architecture-content/chap03.html#tag_03_06_04_06

10. https://pubs.opengroup.org/togaf-standard/architecture-content/chap03.html#tag_03_06_05_07

11. https://pubs.opengroup.org/togaf-standard/architecture-content/chap03.html#tag_03_06_04_09

12. https://pubs.opengroup.org/togaf-standard/architecture-content/chap03.html#tag_03_06_03_05

13. https://pubs.opengroup.org/togaf-standard/architecture-content/chap03.html#tag_03_06_03_04

business functions within the enterprise

(iv) Application Communication Diagram[15] : To depict all models and mappings related to communication between applications in the metamodel entity

Looking at answer choice D :

(i) Actor/Role Matrix[16] : To show which actors perform which roles, supporting definition of security and skills requirements. : **Matches P)**

(ii) System/Technology Matrix[17] : Documents the mapping of applications to technology platform **Matches Q)**

(iii) Goal/Objective/Service Diagram[18] : To define the ways in which a business service contributes to the achievement of a business vision or strategy : **Matches T)**

(iv) Product Life Cycle Diagram[19] : Shows the possible state transitions of a business product, from its creation or receipt to its sale, disposal, or destruction : **Matches S)**

(v) Data Security Diagram[20] : Shows which data is accessed by which roles, organization units, and applications : **Matches R)**

Conclusion and Answer :

Go through all four Observations.

Based on degree of matching, as discussed above :

Best answer : D

Second best answer : A

Third best answer : B

Worst answer : C

---

14. https://pubs.opengroup.org/togaf-standard/architecture-content/chap03.html#tag_03_06_03_04

15. https://pubs.opengroup.org/togaf-standard/architecture-content/chap03.html#tag_03_06_05_07

16. https://pubs.opengroup.org/togaf-standard/architecture-content/chap03.html#tag_03_06_03_13

17. https://pubs.opengroup.org/togaf-standard/architecture-content/chap03.html#tag_03_06_06_03

18. https://pubs.opengroup.org/togaf-standard/architecture-content/chap03.html#tag_03_06_03_21

19. https://pubs.opengroup.org/togaf-standard/architecture-content/chap03.html#tag_03_06_03_20

20. https://pubs.opengroup.org/togaf-standard/architecture-content/chap03.html#tag_03_06_04_07

SQ 214

You are the Lead Enterprise Architect in a company that specializes in the development of wind turbine blades for use in large-scale commercial wind energy production systems. The company has manufacturing facilities located in Illinois, Nebraska, and Manitoba. Each of these plants supplies a different manufacturer that builds and sells complete systems.

The turbine blades are custom engineered to meet each manufacturer's design specifications.

Until recently, most turbine blades were fabricated manually using moulded fibre reinforced plastics. However, recent improvements in composite materials, coupled with enhanced automated methods for precision application of materials during the moulding process, have led to significant reduction in weight, increase in strength, and improved blade longevity.

The company has pioneered the development of a proprietary automated process for continuous extrusion of the turbine blades. Patents have been filed to protect the process, but certain trade secrets must be closely guarded.

The company has a mature enterprise architecture organization that is supported by a cross- functional Architecture Board. The Chief Information Officer and the Chief Operating Officer co- sponsor the enterprise architecture program.

TOGAF® and its Architecture Development Method (ADM) are used to develop the automated manufacturing processes and systems that are used to design, manufacture, and test the blade assemblies.

Recently, a sample architecture project was completed at a single location that defined a standard approach for controlling the Automated Test System that is used at each plant to perform final quality assurance tests on each completed blade assembly.

The Architecture Board approved the plan for immediate implementation at each plant.

Architecture Contracts have been developed that detail the work needed to implement and deploy the new Automated Test System controller for each location. The Chief Engineer, sponsor of the activity, has expressed concern that a uniform process be employed at each location to ensure consistency.

You have been asked to recommend the best approach to address the Chief Engineer's concern. Based on TOGAF® version 10, which of the following is the best answer ?

A : You review the applicable Architecture Contract for each location, ensuring that it addresses the project objectives, effectiveness metrics, acceptance criteria, and risk management. In cases where the contract is issued to an external party, you ensure that it is a legally enforceable contract.

You schedule compliance reviews at key points in the implementation process to ensure that the work is proceeding in accordance with the Architecture Definition. You ensure that the Architecture Board reviews all deviations from the

Architecture Contract, and considers whether or not to grant a dispensation to allow the implementation organization to customize the process to meet their local needs.

B : You create an Architecture Contract to manage and govern the implementation and migration process at each location. For internal development projects, you issue a memorandum of understanding between the Architecture Board and the implementation organization. For contracts issued to an external party, you ensure that it is a fully enforceable legal contract.

You ensure that the Architecture Board reviews all deviations from the Architecture Contract, and considers whether or not to grant a dispensation to allow the implementation organization to customize the process to meet their local needs.

C : You create an Architecture Contract to manage and govern the implementation and migration process.

If the contract is issued to an external party, you ensure that it is a fully enforceable legal contract. For internal development projects, you decided that it is adequate to utilize a memorandum of understanding between the Architecture Board and the implementation organization.

You recommend that if a deviation from the Architecture Contract is detected, the Architecture Board grant a dispensation to allow the implementation organization the ability to customize the process to meet their local needs.

D : You use the issued Architecture Contracts to manage the architecture governance processes for the project across the locations. You deploy monitoring tools to assess the performance of the completed blade assembly at each location and develop change requirements if necessary.

You recommend that if a deviation from the contract is detected, the Architecture Board should modify the Architecture Contract to allow the implementation organization the ability to customize the process to meet their local needs. As a result, you then issue a new Request for Architecture Work to implement the modified Architecture Definition.

Proceeding to tackle the question and getting full five marks :

This Scenario Description appears to be highly (Mechanical) engineering oriented. But if we remember what all to ignore and what all to focus on, there will not be any confusion.

Issues in focus :

Architecture Contracts have been developed that detail the work needed to implement and deploy the new Automated Test System controller for each location.

Aim :

Goal is to replace the functionality of the existing applications with a new product.

To do :

To recommend the best approach to address the Chief Engineer's concern : that a uniform process be employed at each location to ensure consistency : This is related to Implementation Governance and Architecture Contracts.

Important point to note : Architecture Board approved the plan – this means, Phase F is complete and the code development and physical Implementation are about to start.

This is a clue that Contracts are available and that they need be reviewed rather than going for fresh creation.

Remember from Phase G that Governance is closely related to the concept of Architecture Contracts. The drafting of the Contracts start towards end of Phase F.

10. Phase F: Migration Planning

[1]

Enterprise Architecture Capability and Governance
5. Architecture Contracts

[2]

Contracts, in turn are related to ACR – Architectural Compliance Review.

Looking at answer choice A :

You **review the applicable Architecture Contract** for each location, **ensuring that it addresses the project objectives, effectiveness metrics, acceptance criteria, and risk management.** In cases where the contract is issued to an external party, you **ensure that it is a legally enforceable contract.**

You **schedule compliance reviews at key points in the implementation process** to ensure that the work is proceeding in accordance with the Architecture Definition.

You ensure that the **Architecture Board reviews all deviations from the Architecture Contract,** and considers **whether or not to grant a dispensation** to allow the implementation organization to customize the process to meet their local needs.

Points are in line with drawing up of Architecture Contracts in Phase G, ACR – Architecture Compliance Review is suitably described.

Looking at answer choice B :

You **create an Architecture Contract** to manage and govern the implementation and migration process at each location.

For internal development projects, you *issue a memorandum of understanding between the Architecture Board and the implementation organization.*

This has to be a Contract as per ADM, not a document of mere understanding.

1. https://pubs.opengroup.org/togaf-standard/adm/chap10.html

2. https://pubs.opengroup.org/togaf-standard/ea-capability-and-governance/chap05.html

For contracts issued to an external party, you ensure that it is a fully **enforceable legal contract.**

You ensure that the **Architecture Board reviews all deviations from the Architecture Contract,** and considers **whether or not to grant a dispensation** to allow the implementation organization to customize the process to meet their local needs.

The **points above are in line with Phase G, ACR** – Architecture Compliance Review.

Looking at answer choice C :

You **create an Architecture Contract** to manage and govern the implementation and migration process.

If the contract is issued to an external party, you ensure that it is a **fully enforceable legal contract.**

For internal development projects, you decided that it *is adequate to utilize a memorandum of understanding between the Architecture Board and the implementation* organization. *This has to be a Contract as per ADM, not a document of mere understanding.*

You ensure that the **Architecture Board reviews all deviations from the Architecture Contract**, and considers **whether or not to grant a dispensation** to allow the implementation organization to customize the process to meet their local needs.

The **points are in line with Phase G, ACR** – Architecture Compliance Review.

Looking at answer choice D :

You use the issued *Architecture Contracts to manage the architecture governance processes* for the project across the locations. *The Contracts mentioned in Phase G are for 'governing implementation'. Not for entire Architecture Governance.*

You **deploy monitoring tools** to assess the performance of the completed blade assembly at each location and develop change requirements if necessary. *This is an ongoing activity as described in Phase H. This has nothing to do with current scenario and the issue.*

You recommend that if a deviation from the contract is detected, the Architecture Board should modify the Architecture Contract to allow the implementation organization the ability to customize the process to meet their local needs. As a result, you then *issue a new Request for Architecture Work* to implement the modified Architecture Definition. *Dispensation does not lead to a fresh Preliminary Phase and issuance of new Request for Architecture Work.*

Conclusion and Answer :

Go through all four Observations.

Best answer : A

As noted already in the clues, Architecture Board approved the plan – this means, Phase F is complete and the Development and Implementation are about to start. This means that Contracts are available and that they need be reviewed rather than going for fresh creation

Disaster answer : D

Second best and Third best answers will lie between answer choices B and C. When you prepare for the certification, always aim to just reach the best answer. Nothing else other than that should draw your attention

FreshFruit Int. is an online American grocer. The Executive Board decided to implement a new strategy to expand the business to other markets.

The CIO is sponsoring an enterprise activity to support the expanded operations.

A new solution is rolled-out to replace the legacy online sales platform. A compliance review was performed to assess the solution implementation.

The result of the review highlighted a complaint from the development Team stating that the new system is difficult to integrate with the existing warehouse automation systems. The Chief Architect is concerned that the complaint is not related to a real problem of the solution but is based on personal preferences of the development Teams. Another interview with the project Team is scheduled.

You are the Lead Architect and an architect from your Team leads the review Team. You have to answer how, based on TOGAF® you should enable the review Team to conduct the reviews successfully.

Choose one of the following answers :

A : Meeting with the project architect you clarify the purpose of the review. You ask to perform an objective and fair review using the checklists to frame the review and clarify that you want them to identify the issues behind the implementation Team complaints.

B : You organize a meeting with the review Team and state the importance to identify any non-compliancy that may have come from the implemented solution.

C : You organize a meeting with the review Team and stress the importance of a high degree of compliance without any exception. The review should cover every aspect of the implementation and should criticize the implementation techniques.

D : You verify that criteria for the program and the business objectives are mapped in the checklists that the project Team prepared for the interviews. You confirm the checklist content to the project architect and stress the need to be objective and fair during the review process.

Proceeding to tackle the question and getting full five marks :

What to refer :

Enterprise Architecture Capability and Governance
6. Architecture Compliance

1

Looking at answer choice A :

Meeting **with the project architect you clarify the purpose of the review.** You **ask to perform an objective and fair review using the checklists** to frame the review and clarify that *you want them to identify the issues behind the implementation Team complaints.*

While some points are correct, *involvement of EA along with the project architect is underplayed.*

Looking at answer choice B :

You organize a meeting with the review Team and state the importance to identify any non-compliancy that may have come from the implemented solution.

Merely organizing and stating the importance does not take the activity to the required depth.

Looking at answer choice C :

You *organize a meeting with the review Team and stress the importance* of a high degree of compliance without any exception. The **review should cover every aspect of the implementation and should criticize the implementation techniques.**

Just goes one more action of saying what the review will contain, as compared to Answer Choice B.

Looking at answer choice D :

You verify **that criteria for the program and the business objectives are mapped in the checklists** that the project Team **prepared for the interviews.** You **confirm the checklist content to the project architect** and stress the need to be objective and fair during the review process. All are in tune with : 6.4 Architecture Compliance Review Process[2] and the Role and Steps given therein.

Conclusion and Answer :

Go through all four Observations.

Based on above discussion,

Best answer : D

Second best answer : A

---

1. https://pubs.opengroup.org/togaf-standard/ea-capability-and-governance/chap06.html

2. https://pubs.opengroup.org/togaf-standard/ea-capability-and-governance/chap06.html#tag_06_04

Third best answer : C

Worst answer : B

SQ 216

The Architectural Project started in Vision Phase and has successfully completed all iterations and all versions under Phase B, C and D, through what is popularly called BDAT (Business, Data, Application and Technology). Which could be the best answer that suggests the steps needed well before arriving at final Migration and Development decision.

A : The EA would examine the architecture work as available as of date. EA will ensue that the Architectural work is complete as per scope and the descriptions and diagrams and other artifacts are accurate and that they are addressing all known gaps. EA will have to very specifically look into all functional requirements as also all integration requirements. EA has to further ensure that all dependencies are understood and are well documented. Next task would be to create the necessary and additional artifacts in the form of major work packages and transition architectures. At this stage the project charters for the recommended projects are also prepared.

B : The EA would examine the architecture work as available as of date. EA will prioritize projects to transition the organization from the current architecture to target architecture. This will include a business value for each project, the resources required and the intended timing. EA would then validate the prioritizations with the board particularly looking at cost benefits and risks. Finally, EA would generate the Architecture Implementation Roadmap and document lessons learned.

C : EA would assess the requirements of the organization particularly those requirements describing the functions required and information flows within the architecture. EA would then ask the Team to produce artifacts that describe the recommended projects. This would also include Gap Analysis based artifacts to move current architecture to the recommended target architectures. EA would present recommendations to the board for agreement at the end of every Phase. Once this is done, EA would ask the architects to start developing the code.

D : EA would look at the corporate culture and attitude to change, understanding the constraints and on necessary skill sets. EA will determine Business Constraints for Implementation. EA will ensure that the Architectural work is complete as per scope and the descriptions and diagrams and other artifacts are accurate and that they are addressing all known gaps. EA will have to very specifically look into all functional requirements as also all integration requirements. EA to review Consolidated Requirements Across Related Business Functions. EA has to further ensure that all dependencies are understood and are well documented. EA will review and ensure the Readiness and Risk for Business Transformation. Next task would be to create the necessary and additional artifacts in the form of major work packages and transition architectures. At this stage the project charters for the recommended projects are also prepared.

Proceeding to tackle the question and getting full five marks :

We need to identify the portion of TOGAF documentation (available online during Level 2 Exam) so that we can quickly go to that portion and focus only on that. Not more than half a minute to be spent on this.

See the phrase : "steps needed well before arriving at final Migration and Development decision". This is the first clue that question is about Phase E, since that is the Phase that is just before Phase F : Migration Planning.

Note that Phase E : Opportunities and Solutions is "initial Migration Planning while Phase F is "final" Migration Planning. Further clue is from the four answer choices which keep mentioning the points that are in the steps of Phase E.

9. Phase E: Opportunities & Solutions

Chapter Contents: 9.1 Objectives | 9.2 Inputs | 9.3 Steps | 9.4 Outputs | 9.5 Approach

[1]

Let us open 9.3 Steps (of Phase E: Opportunities & Solutions)

These are :

- 9.3.1 Determine / Confirm Key Corporate Change Attributes
- 9.3.2 Determine Business Constraints for Implementation
- 9.3.3 Review and Consolidate Gap Analysis Results from Phases B to D
- 9.3.4 Review Consolidated Requirements Across Related Business Functions
- 9.3.5 Consolidate and Reconcile Interoperability Requirements
- 9.3.6 Refine and Validate Dependencies
- 9.3.7 Confirm Readiness and Risk for Business Transformation
- 9.3.8 Formulate Implementation and Migration Strategy
- 9.3.9 Identify and Group Major Work Packages
- 9.3.10 Identify Transition Architectures
- 9.3.11 Create the Architecture Roadmap & Implementation and Migration Plan

Looking at answer choice A :

Examining the architecture for completion and accurate and on addressing any gaps.

9.3.3 Review and Consolidate Gap Analysis Results from Phases B to D

Consolidate and integrate ... (created in Phases B to D) and ... inter-dependencies

Looking at functional and integration requirements.

9.3.5 Consolidate and Reconcile Interoperability Requirements

Consolidate the ... identified in previous phases

Ensuring that all dependencies are understood and documented.

9.3.6 Refine and Validate Dependencies

Refine the ..., ensuring that ... are identified

---

1. https://pubs.opengroup.org/togaf-standard/adm/chap09.html

Create major work packages and transition architectures and the project charters.

9.3.9 Identify and Group Major Work Packages

Key ...... should assess the ..... identified in the ... and ...

Using the .... matrix together with the ... matrix, logically group the .... into ..

But points missed out include:

Key Corporate Change Attributes

Business Constraints for Implementation

Consolidated Requirements Across Related Business Functions

Readiness and Risk for Business Transformation

Implementation and Migration Strategy

Identifying Transition Architectures (**Very important point**)

Observation : Points mentioned are fine, but missed points include important ones too.

Looking at answer choice B :

The EA would examine the architecture work as available as of date. **True.** But the examination of Consolidated *Gap Analysis Results from Phases B to D is more important and is a specific point that is missing here*

EA will prioritize projects to **transition the organization from the current architecture to target architecture**. Partly correct. See 9.3.10 below

9.3.10 Identify Transition Architectures : Development of Transition Architectures must be based upon the ...., the ... matrix, the listing of .., as well as the enterprise's capacity for .... change.

This will include a business value for each project, the resources required and the intended timing. These are steps in Phase F whereas this question is on a Phase prior to that

EA would then validate the prioritizations with the board particularly looking at cost benefits and risks. These are steps in Phase F and Board is not directly involved in these

Finally, EA would generate the Architecture Implementation Roadmap and document lessons learned. These are steps in Phase F

But points missed out include :

Key Corporate Change Attributes

Business Constraints for Implementation

Consolidated Requirements Across Related Business Functions

Readiness and Risk for Business Transformation

Implementation and Migration Strategy

Observation : Steps mentioned are more for Phase F. Only a partly correct answer seen here. Missed points have been noted.

Looking at answer choice C :

EA would assess the requirements of the organization particularly those requirements describing the functions required and information flows within the architecture. EA would then ask the Team to produce artifacts that describe the recommended projects. This would also include Gap Analysis based artifacts to move current architecture to the recommended target architectures. Every point here is performed in Phases B to D while the present question is on Phase E

EA would present recommendations to the board for agreement at the end of every Phase. Not True. Board is brought into picture only for a final approval

Once this is done, EA would ask the architects to start developing the code. Not True. As per TOGAF, it is the PMO – Project Management Office which will look into actual code development issues, with Architects producing the design only and then playing only as an oversight role during Phase G

Observation : Every point is wrong.

Looking at answer choice D :

EA would look at the corporate culture and attitude to change, understanding the constraints and on necessary skill sets. EA will determine Business Constraints for Implementation. EA will ensue that the Architectural work is complete as per scope and the descriptions and diagrams and other artifacts are accurate and that they are addressing all known gaps. EA will have to very specifically look into all functional requirements as also all integration requirements. EA to review Consolidated Requirements Across Related Business Functions. EA has to further ensure that all dependencies are understood and are well documented. EA will review and ensure the Readiness and Risk for Business Transformation. Next task would be to create the necessary and additional artifacts in the form of major work packages and transition architectures. At this stage the project charters for the recommended projects are also prepared.

Why is every point marked as positive ? Because it matches the following:

- 9.3.1 Determine / Confirm Key Corporate Change Attributes
- 9.3.2 Determine Business Constraints for Implementation
- 9.3.3 Review and Consolidate Gap Analysis Results from Phases B to D
- 9.3.4 Review Consolidated Requirements Across Related Business Functions
- 9.3.5 Consolidate and Reconcile Interoperability Requirements
- 9.3.6 Refine and Validate Dependencies
- 9.3.7 Confirm Readiness and Risk for Business Transformation
- 9.3.8 Formulate Implementation and Migration Strategy
- 9.3.9 Identify and Group Major Work Packages
- 9.3.10 Identify Transition Architectures
- 9.3.11 Create the Architecture Roadmap & Implementation and Migration Plan

Observation : Matches Phase E steps in full.

Conclusion and Answer :

Go through all four Observations.

Best answer : D

Every point therein is correct and matches TOGAF documentation for steps in Phase E

A : Second best answer.

Points answered are fine, but a few missing points

B : Third best answer.

Only partly correct answer found

C : This is a distractor; every point is out of the situations for the question

SQ 217

Patterns & Co. is introducing a Commercial Off-the-Shelf (COTS) Market Analytics solution in order to improve its new delivery service.

Patterns & Co. has a mature enterprise architecture capability and the CIO is the sponsor of the enterprise architecture Team. The business vision and requirements for the new system are defined. It includes a detailed business process analysis. The supplier has proposed a solution but the Architecture Board identified some of the project requirements not consistent with the adopted infrastructure standards. The proposal involved a non-standard Microservice hosting using a Container that does not follow the OCI – Open Container Image standards. The CIO still considered the risks and approved the implementation.

The CIO has asked the EA Team to execute the Phase G ensuring that the system performance KPIs are respected, the project remains within budget and security guidelines are met.

As Lead Enterprise Architect you have to recommend a plan to implement the CIO decision. Choose the best answer according to TOGAF®.

A : You ask the supplier to modify the hardware and software components so they can meet the requisite Container infrastructure standards. Your advise is to come up with a proof of concept to showcase that the modified setup meets the existing standard. Once the agreement with the development leads for supporting the modified architecture, you will provide the project plan to the project manager and also develop an Architecture Contract, the one with the Development Partners, known as Development Service Contract. This is to be followed by frequent reviews at the operational front. The expectation is that such a review can lead to regular monitoring of the production level performance, when scheduled after the implementation is completed and the implementation is handed over to the Line Of Business.

B : You recommend that there will be a co-existence of a second Container standard along with existing one. You set to modify the company Standards Library by adding this new technology of a different one which is not-in-conformance-with-OCI. You would, at this stage, ask the Team of architects to come up with an Architecture Contract with the development Teams, known as Development Service Contract. You also see the need of a performance testing and a compliance review, based on such a Contract. You will have another Contract, the Business Service Contract with the Line Of Business, which focusses on SLAs to be met and also the delivery dates to be adhered to. You further go to identify re-usable procedures and objects based on the additionally introduced standard for Microservice Container images.

C : You will straightaway declare to eliminate the non-standard proposal at this stage itself. Thus the solution as recommended by the Architecture Board will be dropped. You will now create a revised plan and come up with a fresh Architecture Contract which emphasizes for the re-use of standard and existing technologies. This in turn will involve additional cost. You bring up the budget implication of this approach with the finance committee. The CIO will also be apprised by you on the long term cost benefits of this decision. You will ensure the occurrence of regular project management meetings to monitor compliance based on this approach.

D : You will order the team to carry out a risk analysis. You will parallelly set deliverables and timing requirements with the development Team. You will further prepare a detailed impact analysis of the solution chosen. Based on these actions, you will draw up Architecture Contracts, one with Line Of Business and other with the Development Team. You will seek the approval of the CIO at this stage before the proposal goes for implementation. You will line up for proper testing of the solution, to be carried out once the implementation is over. On its successful testing action, you can finally deliver the artifacts relating to this project to the Architecture Landscape portion of the Architecture Repository.

Proceeding to tackle the question and getting full five marks :

What to refer :

Enterprise Architecture Capability and Governance
3. Architecture Governance

[1]

3.2.1 Architecture Governance Framework — Conceptual Structure[2]

See : Under : 3.2.1.2 Key Architecture Governance Processes

Dispensation (also known as Waiver)

A Compliance Assessment can be .... where the subject area (....) are not .... In this case the subject area can :

1. Be ...or r... in order to meet the ...
2. Request a ....

Looking at answer choice A :

You ask the supplier to **modify the hardware and software components** so they can meet the requisite Container infrastructure standards. Your advise is to come up with a proof of concept to showcase that the modified setup meets the existing standard. Once the agreement with the development leads for supporting the modified architecture, you will provide the project plan to the project manager and also develop an Architecture Contract, the one with the Development Partners, known as Development Service Contract. This is to be followed by frequent reviews at the operational front. The expectation is that such a review can lead to regular monitoring of the production level performance, when scheduled after the implementation is completed and the implementation is handed over to the Line Of Business.

This negates all the steps taken form Vision stage onwards, just because of non-compliance of a portion.

Even though the Contract and review portion may sound to be ok, the idea of modification does not gel with the

---

1. https://pubs.opengroup.org/togaf-standard/ea-capability-and-governance/chap03.html

2. https://pubs.opengroup.org/togaf-standard/ea-capability-and-governance/index.html

situation described in the scenario of the question.

Looking at answer choice B :

You recommend that there will be a co-existence of a second Container standard along with existing one. You set to modify the company Standards Library by adding this new technology of a different one which is not-in-conformance-with-OCI. You would, at this stage, ask the Team of architects to come up with an Architecture Contract with the development Teams, known as Development Service Contract. You also see the need of a performance testing and a compliance review, based on such a Contract. You will have another Contract, the Business Service Contract with the Line Of Business, which focusses on SLAs to be met and also the delivery dates to be adhered to. You further go to identify re-usable procedures and objects based on the additionally introduced standard for Microservice Container images.

Fits well within the Dispensation option.

All steps relating to the Contract, SLA formulation and addition of re-usable architecture appear to be fine. The idea that it violates a standard does not mean it has to be rejected at this stage and the Board can think of dispensation. The EA Team is well within its right to add standards conditionally or unconditionally when it is felt necessary.

Looking at answer choice C :

You will straightaway declare to eliminate the non-standard proposal at this stage itself. Thus the solution as recommended by the Architecture Board will be dropped. You will *now create a revised plan and come up with a fresh Architecture Contract* which emphasizes for the re-use of standard and existing technologies. This in turn will involve additional cost. You bring up the budget implication of this approach with the finance committee. The CIO will also be apprised by you on the long term cost benefits of this decision. You will ensure the occurrence of regular project management meetings to monitor compliance based on this approach.

Eliminating like this is only a partial solution and will demand its own time frame to get the new system up and running. Not the best solution under the circumstances.

Looking at answer choice D :

You will order the team to carry out a risk analysis. You will parallelly set deliverables and timing requirements with the development Team. You will further prepare a detailed impact analysis of the solution chosen. Based on these actions, you will draw up Architecture Contracts, one with Line Of Business and other with the Development Team. You will seek the approval of the CIO at this stage before the proposal goes for implementation. You will line up for proper testing of the solution, to be carried out once the implementation is over. On its successful testing action, you can finally deliver the artifacts relating to this project to the Architecture Landscape portion of the Architecture Repository.

The solution portion is re-visited. This option is acceptable only if the roadmap allows for this. Cannot be accepted as the best answer for the situation.

Nevertheless the positive points to be noted here includes risk analysis, impact analysis and so on.

Conclusion and Answer :

Go through all four Observations.

Based on above discussion,

Best answer : B

Second best answer : D

Third best answer : C

Worst answer : A

SQ 218

RIG Networks, a global network supplier is implementing a massive replacement of its supply chain to reduce production cost of their new 5G – 6G bridge gateways. As part of this renovation process the CIO decided to replace their ERP (Enterprise Resource Planning) system using a greenfield approach (where the design the solution, she then identified the suppliers and asked you as Chief Architect to supervise the definition of the Architecture Design and Development Contract.

You now need to write the Architecture Design and Development Contract, identify how you would do this following TOGAF®

Choose one of the following answers :

A : You would define the Architecture Design and Development Contract with : introduction and background, the nature of the agreement, scope of the architecture, architecture and strategic principles and requirements, conformance requirements, Target Architecture Measures, Defined phases of deliverables, Prioritized joint workplan, Time window, Architecture delivery and business metrics.

B : You would define the Architecture Design and Development Contract with : introduction and background, the nature of the agreement, scope of the architecture, architecture and strategic principles and requirements, conformance requirements, Baseline Architecture definition, Target Architecture Measures, Define phases of deliverables, Prioritized joint workplan, Time window, Architecture delivery and business metrics.

C : You would define the Architecture Design and Development Contract with : Target Architecture Measures, Define phases of deliverables, Prioritized joint workplan, Time window, Architecture delivery and business metrics.

D : You would define the Architecture Design and Development Contract with : scope, goals, objectives and constraints, Architecture Principles, Baseline Architecture, Architecture Models, Gap Analysis, Impact Assessment.

Proceeding to tackle the question and getting full five marks :

To do

To supervise the definition of the Architecture Design and Development Contract. This is the contact with the Development Partners.

What to refer :

Enterprise Architecture Capability and Governance
5. Architecture Contracts

1

Typical contents of an Architecture Design and Development Contract are :

a) Introduction and background

b) The nature of the agreement

c) Scope of the architecture

d) Architecture and strategic principles and requirements

e) Conformance requirements

f) Architecture development and management process and roles

g) Target architecture measures

h) Defined phases of deliverables

i) Prioritized joint workplan

j) Time window(s)

k) Architecture delivery and business metrics

As seen in :

Architecture Content
4. Architecture Deliverables

2

4.2.2 Architecture Contract[3]

Looking at answer choice A :

You would define the Architecture Design and Development Contract with : **introduction and background, the nature of the agreement, scope of the architecture, architecture and strategic principles and requirements,**

---

1. https://pubs.opengroup.org/togaf-standard/ea-capability-and-governance/chap05.html

2. https://pubs.opengroup.org/togaf-standard/architecture-content/chap04.html

3. https://pubs.opengroup.org/togaf-standard/architecture-content/chap04.html#tag_04_02_02

conformance requirements, Target Architecture Measures, Defined phases of deliverables, Prioritized joint workplan, Time window, Architecture delivery and business metrics.

By and large, necessary points are covered.

Looking at answer choice B :

You would define the Architecture Design and Development Contract with : **introduction and background, the nature of the agreement, scope of the architecture, architecture and strategic principles and requirements, conformance requirements,** *Baseline Architecture definition,* **Target Architecture Measures, Defined phases of deliverables, Prioritized joint workplan, Time window, Architecture delivery and business metrics.**

Point about Baseline Architecture definition is not correct.

Looking at answer choice C :

You would define the Architecture Design and Development Contract with : **Target Architecture Measures, Defined phases of deliverables, Prioritized joint workplan, Time window, Architecture delivery and business metrics.jn nnmm**

Points mentioned are correct. *But a few are missing.*

Looking at answer choice D :

You would define the Architecture Design and Development Contract with : scope, goals, objectives and constraints, Architecture Principles, Baseline Architecture, Architecture Models, Gap Analysis, Impact Assessment.

Quite way off than the prescribed content.

Conclusion and Answer :

Go through all four Observations.

Based on the discussion above,

Best answer : A

Second best answer : B

Third best answer : C

Worst answer : D

RAMKI

SQ 219

Dante Manufacturing is a big supplier in the automotive industry, head quartered in London with main plants in New York, Milan, Toronto and Tokyo. Each one of these plants has been operating its own Manufacturing Requirements Planning (MRP II) system, production scheduling and custom applications for production automation. Dante's objective is to minimize waste in production by improving production operations. During an analysis of the process improvements, it was determined that a significant improvement on waste production could be achieved by replacing the outdated MRP-II system with a common Enterprise Resource Planning (ERP) located in London.

Dante has well-developed governance and processes based on TOGAF®. The Chief Engineer of Global Manufacturing operations is the business sponsor and issued a Request for Architectural Work. The architectural activity for the implementation of the new ERP platform is kicked off and the architectural vision is produced. Some concerns on the security, reliability, responsiveness and time to manage change of driving the MRP II and production scheduling by a central system located in London are raised by the Team of architects working on the project and by senior management of the various organizations. These in particular stressed the need to align the information management with the business.

As Lead Architect you have been asked to update the IT architectural principles to address the concerns raised by the project stakeholders and the senior management. According to TOGAF®, which of the following is the best answer ?

Choose one of the following answers :

A. Common Use Applications, Data is Shared, Data is Accessible, Data is Secure, Interoperability, Control, Technology Independence.

B. Business Continuity, Service-Orientation, Data is Shared , Data is Accessible, Data is Secure, Responsive Change Management.

C. Requirements-Based Change, Ease-of-Use, Data is Normalized.

D. Information Management is Everybody's business, IT Responsibility, Data Trustee, Technology Independence, Responsive Change Management.

Proceeding to tackle the question and getting full five marks :

What to refer :

ADM Techniques
2. Architecture Principles

Situation : Going for common Enterprise Resource Planning (ERP)

Request for Architectural Work, Architectural Vision are produced

Concerns are on :

Security

Reliability

Responsiveness in time to manage change

Looking at answer choice A :

Common Use Applications

Data is Shared

Data is Accessible

Data is Secure : To address concern on Security

Interoperability

Control

Technology Independence

Looking at answer choice B :

Business Continuity

Service-Orientation

Data is Shared

Data is Accessible

Data is Secure : To address concern on Security

Responsive Change Management : To address concerns on topic of the scenario

Looking at answer choice C :

Requirements-Based Change

---

1. https://pubs.opengroup.org/togaf-standard/adm-techniques/chap02.html

Ease-of-Use

Data is Normalized

Looking at answer choice D :

Information Management is Everybody's business : Leads to Reliability from overall perspective

IT Responsibility : Leads to Reliability from IT perspective

Data Trustee : To address concern on Security, but from a higher plane

Technology Independence

Responsive Change Management : To address concerns on topic of the scenario

Conclusion and Answer :

Go through all four Observations.

Based on the discussion above, and counting the number of principles that address the concerns,

Best answer : D

Second best answer : B

Third best answer : A

Worst answer : C

SQ 220

You are serving as the Lead Architect for a telecommunications company that recently formed through the merging of three other telecommunication companies. The business operating model has been unified, and an enterprise architecture program has been put in place to manage the integration of the three organizations.

The company has adopted the TOGAF® Architecture Development Method. It has successfully completed the architecture definition phases of an ADM cycle and has identified a large collection of candidate roadmap components. The CIO is the sponsor of the program. She is concerned about the risks to the existing revenue lines and would also like to ensure that the most cost-beneficial projects are undertaken first.

The Architecture Board has approved the draft Architecture Definition Document and they are now at the stage of conducting migration planning. A working group has been formed that involves all the key architects and the stakeholders from the corporate matrix (those who will work on the project).

You have been asked to recommend how they can identify and prioritize the projects from these roadmap components, taking account of the CIO's concerns.

Based on the TOGAF® Standard, which of the following is the best answer ?

A : Use the Implementation Factor Assessment and Deduction Matrix to document factors impacting the Migration Plan; use the Consolidated Gaps, Solutions, and Dependencies Matrix to consolidate the gaps from Phases B, C, and D; use the Transition Architecture State Evolution Table to show the proposed state of the architectures at various levels; use the Business Value Assessment Technique to analyze the relative value and risk of each proposed project; and use the Architecture Definition Increments Table to show the proposed series of Transition Architectures.

B : Determine the key corporate change attributes; determine the business constraints; review and consolidate gap analysis results from Phases B, C, and D; review requirements; consolidate interoperability requirements; refine and validate dependencies; confirm readiness and risk for business transformation; formulate the Implementation and Migration Strategy; identify and group major work packages; identify Transition Architectures; create roadmap and plan.

C : Review and consolidate the gap analysis results from Phases B, C, and D by making use of the Consolidated Gaps, Solutions, and Dependencies Matrix. Rationalize the gap analysis and identify dependencies. Group the activities into a coherent set of projects. Use the Business Value Assessment Technique to assign a business value to each project, taking account of value and risk factors. Prioritize the projects into a Migration Plan taking account of dependencies, cost/ benefit analysis, and risk.

D : Create a list of all possible projects from the gap analysis results of Phases B, C, and D. Use the Business Value Assessment Technique to assign a business value to each project, taking account of value and risk factors. Prioritize the projects into a Migration Plan, taking account of dependencies, cost/benefit analysis, and risk. Create an Architecture

Definition Increments Table showing how a series of Transition Architectures may be implemented to achieve the Migration Plan.

Proceeding to tackle the question and getting full five marks :

Issues in focus :

Integration of the Enterprises.

Aims :

Looking into the concerns about the risks to the existing revenue lines and would also like to ensure that the most cost-beneficial projects are undertaken first.

To do :

Select the best among the answer choices based on recommendations on how they can identify and prioritize the projects from these roadmap components, taking account of the CIO's concerns.

Two phases to be looked into :

9. Phase E: Opportunities & Solutions

[1]

10. Phase F: Migration Planning

[2]

Looking at answer choice A :

Use the Implementation Factor Assessment and Deduction Matrix to document factors impacting the Migration Plan; use the Consolidated Gaps, Solutions, and Dependencies Matrix to consolidate the gaps from Phases B, C, and D; use the Transition Architecture State Evolution Table to show the proposed state of the architectures at various levels; use the Business Value Assessment Technique to analyze the relative value and risk of each proposed project; and use the Architecture Definition Increments Table to show the proposed series of Transition Architectures.

This is *less correct* – it uses all the migration planning techniques available but *without showing an understanding of what each technique is used for. It is just a list of the techniques.*

Looking at answer choice B :

Determine the key corporate change attributes; determine the business constraints; review and consolidate gap analysis results from Phases B, C, and D; review requirements; consolidate interoperability requirements; refine and validate dependencies; confirm readiness and risk for business transformation; formulate the Implementation and Migration

---

1. https://pubs.opengroup.org/togaf-standard/adm/chap09.html

2. https://pubs.opengroup.org/togaf-standard/adm/chap10.html

Strategy; identify and group major work packages; identify Transition Architectures; create roadmap and plan.

This is *incorrect*. It is *just a list of the steps of Phase E* but *fails to demonstrate application to the specific scenario which requires use of techniques from Phase F as well as Phase E.*

Looking at answer choice C :

Review and consolidate the gap analysis results from Phases B, C, and D by making use of the Consolidated Gaps, Solutions, and Dependencies Matrix. Rationalize the gap analysis and identify dependencies. Group the activities into a coherent set of projects. Use the Business Value Assessment Technique to assign a business value to each project, taking account of value and risk factors. Prioritize the projects into a Migration Plan taking account of dependencies, cost/benefit analysis, and risk.

This is the **most straightforward approach**, selecting just two of the migration planning techniques, **relevant to project identification and prioritization, risk, and cost/benefit analysis.**

This most addresses the CIO concern of risk and cost/benefit.

Looking at answer choice D :

Create a list of all possible projects from the gap analysis results of Phases B, C, and D. Use the Business Value Assessment Technique to assign a business value to each project, taking account of value and risk factors. Prioritize the projects into a Migration Plan, taking account of dependencies, cost/benefit analysis, and risk. Create an Architecture Definition Increments Table showing how a series of Transition Architectures may be implemented to achieve the Migration Plan.

This is similar to Answer Choice C; **C is slightly better because the Consolidated Gaps, Solutions, and Dependencies Matrix identifies possible duplicated projects earlier** and is a **more rigorous approach than just creating a list of the projects. It also addresses the concerns of risk and cost/benefit analysis.**

Conclusion and Answer :

Go through all four Observations.

Best answer : C

Next best : D

Third best : A

Worst answer : B

About the various Book Series available from the same Author

The three volumes together make up for your preparation for Level 1 Exam – TOGAF® 9.2

This 9.2 Certification is kept open even as TOGAF 10 Certification has started.

Might remain so for quite a few months ahead

TOGAF® 9.2 Level 2

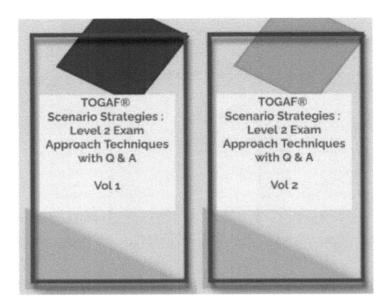

The two volumes together makes up for your preparation for Level 2 Exam – TOGAF® 9.2

Ideally $TOGAF^®$ 10 can be approached with a One hour exam,

if you possess TOGAF® 9.2 or TOGAF® 9.1 Certification

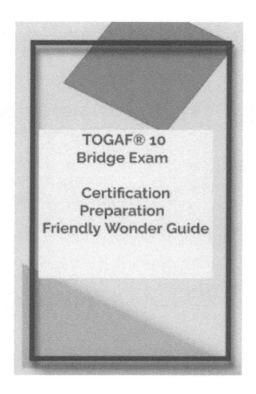

Our Book which can steer you to $TOGAF^®$ 10 through the Bridge Exam

And for those who want to take TOGAF® 10 fresh, our emerging Book Series happen to be :

As also Volumes on Level 2 tilted as Scenario Strategies for TOGAF® 10 Exam

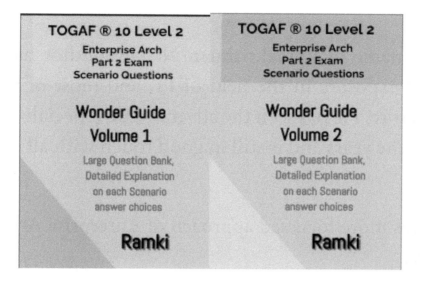

This Book is one among the two

And to be really practical and ready with TOGAF Competence :

Author & Expert Faculty : Ramakrishnan N (Ramki)

Ramki is the pen name of Ramakrishnan N. This author has nearly 50 years of experience and exposure in the field of IT, and most of it is attributed to Software Architecture. He has seen the advent of this specialist field of Software Architecture over the years and is still in good touch with all modern evolution of the same.

TOGAF® 10 places more focussed approach of Enterprise Architecture getting into areas such as :

- Microservice Architecture
- Digital Enterprise and Digital Technology Adoption : Digital Business Reference Model (DBRM)
- Information Mapping and Organization Mapping
- Customer Master Data Management (C-MDM)
- TOGAF® ADM using Agile Sprints

These happen to be the precise areas where the author has equipped himself with practical and conceptual knowledge.

Books of same author, Ramki, as TOGAF® Certification Wonder Books (three volumes for Level 1 and one for Level 2 – Scenario Strategies) have been admired and being purchased by hundreds on a day to day basis.

Books on Design Patterns and other Architectural topics are also to the credit of this author.

He has also provided training to participants from a large number of Enterprises spanning all over the globe. The number of participants to his TOGAF® courses alone is close to 2200 as of mid 2023.

Reachable through: mramkiz@gmail.com

9 798223 987932